LEADING EDGE

Leadership Strategies from the New Testament

Robert D. Dale

ABINGDON PRESS

Nashville

LEADING EDGE:
LEADERSHIP STRATEGIES FROM THE NEW TESTAMENT

Copyright © 1996 by Abingdon Press

This book is printed on recycled, acid-free paper.

Library of Congress Cataloging-in-Publication Data

Dale, Robert D.
    Leading edge: leadership strategies from the New Testament/
Robert D. Dale.
        p.   cm.
    Includes bibliographical references.
    ISBN 0-687-01506-5 (pbk.: alk. paper)
    1. Christian leadership.   2. Leadership in the Bible.   3. Jesus
Christ—Leadership.   I. Title.
BV652.1.D335   1996
253—dc20   96-11267
                                                                        CIP

96 97 98 99 00 01 02 03 04 05 — 10 9 8 7 6 5 4 3 2 1

MANUFACTURED IN THE UNITED STATES OF AMERICA

To
Reginald M. McDonough
who has made leadership strategy
a ministry of passion and compassion
—passion for God's future
and compassion for those who are reluctant to risk

CONTENTS

FREEDOM

The Strategic
Exercise of Ministry

— 1 —
The Edge
Where and How
Leadership Happens

Real leadership happens on the edge, on the boundaries where opportunities and resources meet. On these strategic edges, leaders live by their values and are forced to make delicate choices. Consequently, the most spiritually sensitive, cerebral, and sophisticated level of leadership involves *strategy*. At this highest level, leadership becomes an art—the art of strategy. Thankfully for Christians, the New Testament is a revealing resource on how to develop an effective leadership strategy.

What Is Leadership Strategy?

When I think of "strategy," I think of a distinctive, an "edge," an advantage, or a point of excellence—to be recognized, expanded, and used as a stewardship.[1] Strategy is how religious leaders discover, maintain, and enrich the stewardship of their gifts, abilities, and strengths—their edge.

Simply put, ministry strategy calls for the expansion of excellence. Strategic leaders do their best—even better. Then, they help their organizations do their best—even better. The "edge"—either personal or congregational—grows out of the discovery of what is done best and achieved with excellence. The expansion of the edge, then, challenges us to do more of the best or to do the best at a higher level of excellence.

9

Strategy, consequently, pushes us toward two discoveries: (1) what is my edge for leadership and ministry? and, (2) how can I lead and minister from that edge with excellence? When these basic discoveries are made, the options are dramatically clarified. Positively, we target what we do best and do it better and do more of it. Negatively, we isolate what we do poorly and stop doing it now.

The concepts of strategy were applied first by generals in the ancient Greek army. As a result, the word strategy itself refers to "generalship." In military history as well as in modern society, strategy describes the stewardship of any advantage or edge or strength for future effectiveness.

Who Are Today's Strategists?

Coaches, military leaders, marketing gurus, and planners are some of today's prime strategic thinkers. Dean Smith, head basketball coach at the University of North Carolina at Chapel Hill, is a legend at designing winning strategies, building creative combinations from the unique talents of each year's team, and using the time clock to his team's advantage. During a home game in the 1973–74 season, North Carolina was trailing archrival Duke by eight points with only sixteen seconds left in the game. Smith called time out and announced to his team that they had their opposition right where they wanted them! Smith set the strategy and sent his team back to the court for the finale. Carolina, led by the heroics of Walter Davis and Bobby Jones, made an unbelievable comeback to tie the game at the buzzer on a desperation shot from 35 feet by Davis. Then, Carolina beat Duke in overtime! That's the stuff of strategy—and of legends!

I also like the strategy compliment another leading basketball coach paid Smith. Bobby Knight, the Indiana University coach, said that if he had five minutes to live, he would want Dean Smith to manage the clock! That's a recognition of Smith's strategic artistry.

Strategy as an Issue in Practical Theology

Our era of ministry calls for strategists as leaders. In general, we have more and more opportunities for ministry and fewer and fewer resources for ministry. Practical questions bubble out of the intersection between opportunities and resources in your ministry.

(1) Does your church have more ministry resources than it can use?
(2) Does your church have a bigger budget than it can spend?
(3) Does your church have more trained workers than it can deploy?
(4) Does your church take full advantage of all its ministry opportunities?

If you answered "no" to any or all of these questions, then an answer to more effective leadership is strategy.

As a practical matter, strategy is what you, as a church leader, apply to your ministry when you realize that

you can't be two places at one time,
you can only spend your days and dollars once,
you can only become effective in ministry by using to the maximum the gifts and opportunities God has uniquely given to you, you can only befriend and deeply relate to people one-at-a-time,
you can't do your work or face ministry challenges like anyone else, and
you can't meet every human need or save the entire world singlehandedly.

When you discover the limits of your resources as well as the scope of your opportunities, strategy is demanded for effectiveness. You and your church's other leaders must think and act strategically in order for your church to do its ministry well.

You can apply strategy to your ministry in two ways—individually and congregationally. On an individual basis, you can identify the gifts for ministry God has given you, and then you can commit yourself to grow and to become the best steward of your strengths you can be. Or, from a congregational perspective, you can help your church evaluate its ministry opportunities and resources and then capitalize on its possibilities.

Nathan Bedford Forrest, the famous (and infamous) Confederate military raider, claimed that he won battles simply by getting there "fustest with the mostest." When Forrest arrived first on the field with the most soldiers, he had a distinctive edge,[2] or, more accurately, two edges. "First" and "most" are both leadership resources; they give leaders an edge in strategy effectiveness. Because "first" and "most" are only two of many strategies, we will identify numerous other strategy edges throughout this book.

Why Is Strategy Important?

We live during a time in history when strategy is becoming increasingly important. The old loyalty-based organizations and systems are rapidly being replaced by service-based organizations and systems. With the demise of loyalty-based organizations, people ask what institutions can do for them. We and our neighbors are demanding more, and better, and faster from our organizations.

Tom Peters, in *Liberation Management,* contrasts the A-mode of strategy with the H-mode. The A-mode grows out of the agricultural model of civilization and is characterized by stability, hierarchy, control, and leaders who operate independently. The H-mode of strategy harkens back to the hunter-gatherer epoch in history and is distinguished by movement, flexibility, and leaders who create teamwork.[3]

My Grandpa Kingry learned both the A- and H-modes of strategy quickly when he homesteaded in western Kansas shortly after the turn of this century. Farmers planting first crops knew they had to live off the land until harvest. While Grandpa and his young neighbors adopted the settled

A-mode strategies and rhythms of the farm, they were also forced to adapt themselves to the H-mode lifestyle of the hunt. On those days when the cupboard was bare and supper had to be found before dark, Grandpa and his neighbors hunted antelopes. The young hunters noticed that antelopes were cagey and kept their distance. They also observed that when antelopes were chased, they ran in circles. Twelve young riders on fresh horses could pursue an antelope for a dozen laps, run the weakened animal down, and kill it at the end of the chase. The A-mode farmers, by necessity, used H-mode hunting strategies too.

In our day, according to Tom Peters, the H-mode of strategy is reappearing because it can adapt more easily to radical new needs, opportunities, and demands. The H-mode fits our leadership needs increasingly. When we are faced with chaotic situations, rapid change, unwieldy structures, and rigidly authoritarian leaders, it's an H-mode kind of world! H-modes of living in congregations require strategic thinking and acting rooted solidly in healthy theology.

Theology-Driven Strategy

"Beliefs drive strategy,"[4] claims Tom Chappell, company president and divinity school graduate. Theology undergirds our leadership approach. Or, to state the case more experientially, leadership reveals our operational theology.

Chappell, by the way, practices what he preaches. He has reinvented his company's service philosophy. Since he went to divinity school and discovered the direct connection between believing and behaving, Chappell's company has begun donating 10 percent of its profits to charitable causes. Additionally, Chappell's employees are encouraged to donate 5 percent of their time to community service. Beliefs are reflected in our strategies.

Strategy in Biblical Context

The Bible is a strategy book. Why? Because, in part, it shows how God has "thought strategically" about our salvation. Scripture speaks of the fullness of time, of counting costs, of reaping

13

ripe harvests, and of being called to the Kingdom for such times as these.

God is an "on purpose" God, a strategist. The Lord does nothing haphazardly. God acts intentionally: our salvation was planned by God even before the Creation (1 Peter 1:20). God also works on schedule: Christ was sent to us only after God had ripened the time (Galatians 4:4). When God sent his Son to redeem us, Jesus came to earth with a ministry strategy. God has modeled strategic action for us in Jesus and the leaders of the early church and has called us to follow their examples.

Learning the Craft

Do you suppose that Jesus learned the art and craft of strategy in Joseph's carpentry shop?[5] As apprentice to the village woodworker, Jesus must have learned to visualize a piece of furniture. Imagine a townsman ordering a table for his home from Jesus. First, Jesus "saw" the shape of the table in his mind's eye and custom-designed that specific table. He went into the forest and selected a tree that "contained" the table in his imagination. He cured the lumber and sharpened his tools. He, then, painstakingly and lovingly created the table by sawing and chiseling and planing away all of the wood that didn't "look" like his table. Finally, Jesus took the risk of presenting the finished product to his customer. In other words, carpenters in Jesus' day were strategists, designers, foresters, and woodcrafters who "saw the shape" of a project, devised a plan for producing that result, and step-by-step risked building what they had envisioned and planned. That demanding pattern of strategy development remains the same for today's ministries.

Identifying a Strategy Cycle

If strategy is the adventure of finding an edge and maximizing it, what are the steps in the pattern of strategy development? Visualize a three-step cycle that's a variation on the art of marksmanship: aim, ready, fire. Each step involves a specific leadership action and has its own "punctuation."

14

STRATEGY CYCLE

#1 "AIM ..."/
RESULT EDGE

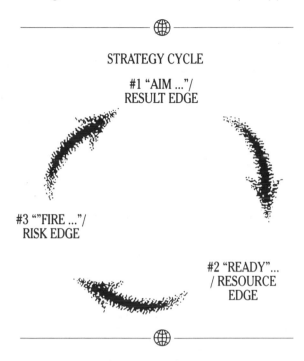

#3 ""FIRE ..."/
RISK EDGE

#2 "READY"...
/ RESOURCE
EDGE

(1) **"Aim ..."** identifies your **"result edge."** "Aim" uses the ellipsis of durative action. "Aim" keeps leaders on target by continuing to raise the question, "What ministry result do we ultimately want to achieve?" The "aim" step in the strategy cycle pinpoints our preferred future, the orbit we hope to attain.

(2) **"Ready?"** ends with a question mark, because it evaluates and mobilizes your **"resource edge."** The "ready" of resource discovery probes the issue, "What do we have to work with in ministry?" The "ready" step in the strategy cycle establishes the launchpad we will use to move into the unknowns of the future.

(3) **"Fire!"** uses an exclamation point, exercising your faith by taking action toward your **"risk edge."** "Fire" reminds leaders that pacesetting requires the risks of faith, initiative, and liftoff. In the final analysis, there's no leadership without action.

The aim/ready/fire cycle keeps leadership strategists on the cutting edge. In utilitarian terms, strategy is taking action toward the right result with the right resources through the right risks.

Strategists can, however, forfeit their edge at any of the three stages of the strategy cycle. For example, some observers of the business scene claim America lost its competitive edge to Japan by neglecting to complete the strategy cycle. These observers note that the American business community tends to follow a "ready, aim, aim, aim, aim" pattern and not take the risks of acting. Have churches also crafted beautiful plans and then neglected to implement their goals?

Aiming for the Target

The first step in strategy development calls us to choose a core vision. Vision provides the "aim" or "result edge" for strategists. This motivating dream becomes our passion, our near-obsession, and our target to pursue. Targeted visions provide the long-range objective, give our actions a track to run on, and show outsiders how to understand our leadership behaviors.

I remember exactly where I was and what I was doing when I discovered Jesus' core vision for his ministry. I was in my study in Lawrence, Kansas, preparing a sermon when my interest was captured by an emphasis in A. M. Hunter's New Testament theology. Hunter claimed that Jesus' life and work were dominated by a central idea.[6] I was sure—whatever Hunter was about to identify for me—I had heard dozens of sermons on the theme, had been taught the finer points of the idea in college and seminary, and had preached and taught the concept myself. To my surprise and shame I had never preached on Jesus' crowning vision. I couldn't remember hearing a sermon or lecture on it either. I realized that if one idea was central to Jesus' thought and I had neglected it, I would never have the mind of Christ in me until I steeped myself in that key idea and let it dominate my thinking too. I've never escaped that flash of insight. I'm still, however, trying to master my Master's vision and core value.

For Jesus, his basic ministry vision was the kingdom of God. That's what Hunter—and God's Spirit—taught me on that watershed day in Kansas. I was driven back to the Gospels with fresh eyes and discovered an amazing trend. Jesus spoke of the kingdom of God more than any other single theme, a total of about eighty references in the Gospels. Most of his striking parables begin with the refrain, "The kingdom of God is like. . . ." Boldly and repeatedly, Jesus calls on us to yield our lives—singly and together—to the rule of God. He challenged us to invite God to be our king. Jesus took the kingdom of God seriously. He lived and died for God's kingdom. It was his motive and his message. Jesus' vision fits new movements and isn't a bureaucratic "technique" that is imposed on group members.

When your aim is steady on your selected target, you must get ready and fire. These two additional steps are essential to the strategy cycle. In other words, you assess your resources and, finally, you take the risks of faith. That completes the strategic cycle by linking results, resources, and risks in action.

Strategy in the Gospels

The New Testament provides us with wholesome models of leadership strategy. For instance, have you ever wondered why the Gospel writers told the same basic story in four distinct ways? Why not assemble a scriptorium—which is a room full of scribes—and make copies of the same story? Because each writer had specific results in mind, had identified the particular resources he had, and was willing to take distinctive risks in sharing his faith. Each of the Gospel writers approaches his witnessing opportunity differently, strategically. Each Gospel illustrates a distinctive leadership strategy for getting the good news out in a particular manner or to a specific audience.[7]

Mark, the earliest of the Gospels to be written, demonstrates a **communication strategy: choose your message and keep it lean and lively.** Sometimes called the "motion picture" Gospel for its fast pace and high energy level, Mark begins with Jesus announcing the kingdom: "The time is fulfilled, and the kingdom of God has come near; repent, and believe in the good news" (Mark 1:15). Mark then moves swiftly straight ahead from powerful event to striking miracle to the Cross and Resurrection. Mark came right to the point and stuck with the kingdom theme all the way through the book. His "keep it simple and swift" approach is what leadership specialists describe as "a bias for action."[8]

Matthew was written to tell the Jews about Jesus. He adopted an **audience strategy: appeal to a specific group.** Matthew obviously addresses the Jews. He begins, for instance, by tracing Jesus' family tree back to Abraham, quotes the Old Testament heavily, and, in passages like the Sermon on the Mount, shows Jesus frequently teaching various groups in the fashion of a Jewish rabbi.

Luke used the flip side of Matthew's strategy. Luke, the only Gentile writer in the New Testament, stressed that Christ had died for all kinds of people in all kinds of places. Consequently, he applied a **global strategy: reach out to new, unreached groups.** Luke spoke more of Samaritans, outcasts, women, and the poor than the other Gospel writers—and often made his point about broad outreach through Jesus' unforgettable parables and metaphors.

John's Gospel depicted another crucial strategy point. John used a **symbolic strategy, aligning works and words.** He structured his story of Jesus around seven "signs," a presentation of miracles followed by theological explanations. John knew the reinforcing power of actions and interpretations—in tandem and in agreement.

A friend told me how important he'd found symbols in leadership. This friend was the chief executive officer of a Texas-based construction company when the southwestern economy soured in the mid-1980s. The company had to pare back on its spending, but no memo or speech seemed to get the message across. My friend decided the company had to be slimmed down. One Monday morning, he eliminated an entire layer of the organization chart by firing all the vice presidents at that level, worldwide. To his dismay, no one got very excited, and, worse yet, no belts tightened. This executive is a savvy leader and decided a symbolic act was called for. After some thought, he hit on the proper action. The company had a huge hunting lease where old customers and new prospects were entertained. The company had several prize hunting dogs on the lease. He sold the dogs! Like a prairie fire, word spread through the company that the corporation really was in financial trouble. Why else would the dogs have to go? Likewise John's Gospel uses symbolic strategies well. Let your works and words link up, and your point is apt to be heard.

The four Gospel writers obviously knew strategy, didn't they? They chose to tell Jesus' story in ways that reflected the result, resource, and risk cycle. The Gospel writers were effective strategists.

The Flow of This Book

This book will develop a practical theology of leadership strategy around four themes: focus, flexibility, future-orientation, and feasibility. First, we will study Jesus in the Gospels as a leader with a focused strategy. Next, we will explore the flexible strategies of Acts and the churches identified in the Epistles. Additionally, we will remind ourselves of the constant need for future-orientation, the key leadership issue in the Pastoral Epistles. Finally, we will briefly survey the theme of feasibility in Revelation, surviving to lead a new strategic cycle after a crisis has been endured. Each of these New Testament case studies illuminates ministry strategy then and now.

At the outset, be forewarned that I'm a nontechnical student of the New Testament. For the purposes of this book only, the filter through which I will view the biblical materials is the interdisciplinary perspective of leadership studies. I will try to read the familiar stories of the New Testament through the lens of leadership and report my impressions to you.

Let's allow the New Testament to instruct us in the art of leadership strategy now. Watch the themes of focus, flexibility, future-orientation, and feasibility emerge.

FOCUS

The Strategic
Stewardship of
Energy

— 2 —
Jesus
Focused Master
Strategist

Like Janus, the patron of beginnings and endings from Roman mythology, the ability to look in two directions is crucial for effective strategists. Why? Because strategy is revealed both by what we turn our faces toward and do as well as by what we turn our backs on and choose not to do. Jesus consistently served the kingdom of God; that's what he did. What he didn't do is made obvious by the decisions he made during his temptations. Jesus' leadership strategy used at least a two-sided approach to the kingdom of God.

Jesus as a Strategist

Jesus' strategies were especially appropriate for the task of launching a new ministry. Remember that each strategy represents an advantage Jesus felt he possessed and could apply to his calling.

To launch the kingdom of God, Jesus focused on defining himself. When Jesus burst upon the pages of the New Testament as the Messiah, he was already about thirty years old. His declaration of his ministry ended nearly two decades of silence in the Gospel record. What had Jesus been doing? To say that he had been working in the carpenter's shop and taking care of his brothers and sisters only tells part of the story. Most importantly, he had been defining himself.

Think about the great religious leaders throughout history—Moses, Jesus, Paul, Luther, Wesley. They didn't undertake the ministries for which we admire them until they were roughly thirty. It takes maturity and "mileage" to prepare us for significant ministry and strategic leadership.

When Jesus launched his ministry, he knew exactly who he was and what he was called to do. The temptations and the "I am" statements of John's Gospel illustrate Jesus' certainty about who he was. Jesus never "lost" himself. Kierkegaard claimed, while lesser losses are usually noticed, life's biggest danger, the danger of losing oneself, can pass off in the world as quietly as if it were nothing.[1] Leaders who are rooted and centered in a clear self-definition work with a distinct advantage and lessen the odds that they will forfeit themselves somewhere along the way.[2]

To launch the kingdom of God, Jesus focused on building a new community. From the Twelve to the common people of the multitudes, Jesus called a distinctive group of persons to himself. For Jesus, this new community became his extended family. Later, these believers would bond together and band together as the church.

To launch the kingdom of God, Jesus focused on training apprentices. Jesus didn't ask his followers to be Christians; he simply invited them to become "disciples," or learners. They were apprenticed to the Master of the kingdom. The Twelve, the seventy, and those who heard the Sermon on the Mount or listened to his parables or observed his miracles were receiving on-the-job training for kingdom building. For kingdom purposes, we're always rookies with more to learn and experience. None of us is ever a "pro" in God's kingdom.

To launch the kingdom of God, Jesus focused on his selected times and places for action. Jesus displayed a keen sense of timing. He knew when his hour had not yet arrived, and he knew when to urge his followers not to announce his messiahship prematurely. He knew when to set his face like a flint toward Jerusalem and face the Cross (Luke 9:51). Jesus also possessed an uncanny sense of place. He went home and risked Nazareth's rejection (Luke 4). He deliberately traveled through Samaritan territory (John 4) in order to show the difference a gospel of love could make to persons of mixed race who had previously only endured prejudice and hate from Jews.

To launch the kingdom of God, Jesus focused on mobilizing his representatives. The seventy were sent out, the Samaritan woman was told to witness to her own village, and the Gerasene demoniac was instructed to go home and show his neighbors how his life had changed.

To launch the kingdom of God, Jesus focused on modeling love. John 3:16 capsulizes God's love for us through Jesus. The Great Commandment instructs us to love God and our neighbors (Matthew 22:37-40). The New Commandment challenges us to love one another (John 13:34-35). Everywhere Jesus went, he modeled love. Have you noticed that Jesus, out of love, broke up every funeral procession he ever encountered?

To launch the kingdom of God, Jesus focused on the risks of success. Faith and risk are near-synonyms. To be faithful requires us to take risks. After all, doesn't missionary history remind us to expect great things from God and to attempt great things for God? If we don't try, we fail for sure. If we do try, the risks we take have the potential to lead us to success.

Say Yes, Say No

We've seen what Jesus did. But we can learn a lot about Christian leadership strategy by identifying the ministry strategies Jesus rejected. The accounts of Jesus' temptations in Matthew 4 and Luke 4 show us that strategy always involves *yes* and *no* choices.

C. S. Lewis tells a powerful story about choosing our lives. He describes a trip some citizens of hell take to heaven for a visit. Each of the travelers is given the chance to enter heaven by giving up his or her besetting sin. Even the preacher who pastors a thriving congregation in hell is given another chance. But, finally everyone chooses to return to hell. It's their choice. As Lewis explains it, "There are only two kinds of people in the end: those who say to God, 'Thy will be done,' and those to whom God says, in the end, 'Thy will be done.' All that are in hell choose it."[3]

25

Ouch! How painfully true Lewis' observation is. Our lives—the hellish parts as well as the heavenly parts—are the products of our strategic choices. Our *yeses* and *no*s have consequences.

Choosing Strategically

We are ultimately as much defined by what we don't choose as by what we do select.[4] Management guru Peter Drucker correctly claims, "The essence of strategy is denial."[5] *Yes* and *no* are always defining decisions.

Opportunity: the Achilles Heel

Strategic choices become even more complicated when we have a myriad of possibilities. Leaders are most likely seduced by opportunity.[6] That is, we are most likely to make strategic blunders when we are evaluating open doors of possibility. And the more options we have in ministry, the more seductive temptation becomes.

The Nature of Temptation

Every temptation of Jesus involved a strategic ploy by the devil. In Matthew's account of the testing of Jesus, the devil is described as a tempter. Is it significant in Matthew 4 that the devil isn't depicted as a confronter or a debater? At least in this instance, the devil didn't take Jesus on directly or head-to-head. The approach here seems more subtle. In Greek grammar the kind of *if* clauses used in this section of Matthew 4 assume a condition to be true. In English, we usually preface these statements with "since" and then raise an issue as a fact unquestioned or established.

The devil uses flanking actions here. These temptations are approached with almost a casual offhandedness by the devil. One interpreter envisions temptation as typically occurring over a relaxed second cup of coffee.[7] The devil didn't dare Jesus with a "You aren't able to . . ." or "You shouldn't . . ." challenge. Rather, the angle of access has a tone of "Under this special circumstance, given this exceptional situation, just this once, why don't you . . . ?" There was no red-hot demand to be selfish and to make God secondary; there was only a "Since this is different, why don't you . . . ?" suggestion.

Ironically, the temptations of Genesis 3 are also temptations to put self ahead of God—in this special circumstance. In Genesis 3:6 the forbidden is pleasurable to sample and taste, would lend experience and power, and is interesting to see. In many ways Matthew 4 and Luke 4 echo Genesis 3. All of these passages show the adversary making the same three basic appeals. Do you suppose these temptations are the only strategies he knows?

Jean Kerr uses a humorous story to make a serious point. She tells about her younger son coming home from church kindergarten in a glum mood. In the school drama, he had been given the role of playing Adam in the Garden of Eden. Failing to see how this event could trigger her son's downcast outlook, Jean Kerr pointed out that Adam was the lead role. The little boy agreed but solemnly noted "the snake has all the lines." When Genesis 3, Luke 4, and Matthew 4 are compared, the slippery tempter uses the same well-worn lines every time. Sadly, these same three old lines continue to work as strategies for evil.[8]

Strategically, the devil tried to capitalize on three potential advantages: (1) Jesus was hungry, physically weakened, and might not be thinking clearly; (2) Jesus was launching a worldwide redemptive ministry and might be eager to make progress quickly; and (3) Jesus had an important message to communicate and might be looking for a way to get his word before the people dramatically. The tempter was obviously ready to try to work for any advantage he could muster.

The Best or Bested?

Jesus' ministry was most at risk when he was tempted in the desert at the outset of his ministry. At that point, potentially he could have taken several roads to inaugurate the kingdom of

God. The temptations were the final step in Jesus' preparation for ministry and demonstrated what he believed about his task in ministry. From many potential "good" options, he chose the one actual "best."

The temptations were also critical for the forces of evil. If Jesus could be defeated or detoured, the kingdom of God would die. If Jesus could be bested at the beginning of his ministry, the entire redemptive process would come unraveled.

Vince Lombardi, the legendary coach of the Green Bay Packers professional football team, used a similar strategy in preparing game plans. He studied the opponent's defensive unit until he could identify their four best defenders. Then, Lombardi designed Green Bay's first six plays of the game to be run directly at those four players. That's right. Lombardi opened the game by directing Green Bay's offense at the strength of his opponent. His theory was simple. Attack the other team's heart. If you can defeat your opponent's best and take away his spirit, you can win every time.[9] No wonder the devil met Jesus in the wilderness before Jesus had ever declared himself!

Luke 4: A Case Study in Focused, Strategic Choices

Luke 4 offers us a case study in strategic choices. The temptations are a strategic tug-of-war. In Luke 4, Jesus rejected three dead-end strategies proposed by the devil before our Lord announced his bedrock strategy for kingdom building.

Remember that strategy helps leaders identify their advantages and expand on them. Temptation, on the other hand, lures us to achieve by shortcut. John McClanahan makes a powerful observation about the devil's approach to tempting Jesus:

> Some of the things . . . the devil offered were not bad in themselves. They were actually goals . . . Jesus did want to pursue. The devil's method of reaching these goals, however, left much to be desired. He is the architect of seeking achievement using every shortcut.[10]

The Seduction of Pleasure

The first temptation tried to seduce Jesus with the shortcut of pleasure. The Scripture tells us that Jesus was on trial in the desolate wilderness for forty days; ate nothing during that time; and at the end of that period, not surprisingly, was hungry. The floor of the desert was covered with small, loaf-shaped stones. The tempter must have pointed out how well Jesus had done during these tests and, because of his hunger, how much he deserved a break today. At this juncture the tempter handed Jesus a stone and encouraged him to turn it into bread miraculously. Jesus could have turned a stone into a loaf in an instant, but he didn't. Later in his ministry, Jesus fed thousands on more than one occasion. Fulfillment of human needs was, after all, a basic part of Jesus' ministry. Yet, in this case, he refused to satisfy his own physical needs. Rather, he answered, "One does not live by bread alone" (Luke 4:4).

Why didn't Jesus adopt this ministry strategy of providing for his material appetites—and the pleasures of others? Why did Jesus later pass up another opportunity to be a meat-and-potatoes Messiah who would lift the spirits of his followers with his teaching and then would feed their bodies with food-multiplying miracles (John 6:1-66)? The tempter would have liked nothing more than for Jesus to live on the level of appetites and to become a prosperity-and-pleasure preacher. But Jesus clearly knew that no ministry based on self-service leads to the kingdom of God. He rejected the seduction of the pleasure-providing strategy.

Do you know Karl Olsson? You may be able to identify with some aspects of his pilgrimage: born into a family of ministers, entered ministry himself and became prominent and successful within his denomination, worked all of his life for his father's birthright and blessing, rose to be the highest-ranking executive and educator in his denomination. What more could a minister want? Karl Olsson wanted a sense of blessing and joy. He read about birthrights in the Old Testament and about banquets and parties in the New Testament. He realized he had missed both the birthright and the banquets. He then resigned his denominational posts; and as he describes it, he accepted God's invitation to "come

29

to the party." The pleasures of position and ease hadn't fulfilled him, but God's grace did.[11]

The Seduction of Power

The second temptation of the devil attempted to seduce Jesus with the shortcut of power. In a moment in time, the tempter showed Jesus all the kingdoms of the world. The devil invited Jesus to pay homage to him as king, in exchange for authority over the world. But Jesus knew that political power had nothing to do with God's kingdom. It was, then, a straightforward decision for him to choose to worship and serve God alone (Luke 4:8). Jesus rejected the possibility of establishing his ministry as a politician—in spite of the common hope that the Messiah would be a warrior in the mode of David who would deliver and avenge Israel. Later, during the triumphal entry, Jesus rode a donkey instead of a warhorse into Jerusalem. Power and politics held no appeal for Jesus. The only kingdom to which Jesus would pledge allegiance was the kingdom of God.

Leaders—even ministry leaders—are regularly tempted to compromise with evil in order to reach their goals. Too often, misguided leaders subscribe to the popular idea that success is only made possible by taking shortcuts. It's the age-old argument that the end justifies the means. This attitude can bless any tactic as acceptable—even in the church—if the outcome can be described as holy or half-holy. But moral goals can't be reached by immoral means.

Robert K. Greenleaf's classic book, *Servant Leadership*, opens with a powerful story. A group of persons are on a journey. Leo, a servant, accompanies the party and, while performing menial chores, sings songs and keeps the group's spirits up. The trip goes well until Leo disappears. Then, the group falls into disarray and finally abandons its journey. The group simply cannot proceed without the servant Leo. One member of the group searches for years and at long last locates Leo. To his surprise, Leo, whom the searcher has only known as a servant, is actually the leader of the organization that had sponsored the group's journey in the first place. The leader is servant first—that's the moral of Greenleaf's story as well as a basic New Testament theme.[12]

Leo's lack of ambition mirrors Jesus' downward mobility in the prologue to John's Gospel. The Word who was God became flesh and pitched his tent in our midst (John 1:1-12). Implicit in Jesus' action is a warning. Beware of ambitious, upwardly mobile leaders. Unlike Jesus, they crave and hoard power. The British historian Lord Acton had it right: "Power tends to corrupt, and absolute power corrupts absolutely."

The Seduction of Parade

The third temptation plotted to seduce Jesus into taking the shortcut of parade and sensationalism. In his final attempt to ensnare Jesus, the devil promised Jesus to get him on the ancient equivalent of the six o'clock news. Picture the tempting scene. Jesus would stand on the brink of the Temple parapet and wait for the curious crowds to gather hundreds of feet below. Then, when all eyes were fixed on him, he would do a swan dive and free-fall without a bungee cord. Gasps of horror and surprise would rise involuntarily from the onlookers. Just short of the ground, Jesus would screech to a halt, caught by angels in a heavenly safety net as promised in Psalm 91:11-12. At least that's the way the tempter envisioned the event. Think of the coverage that kind of magic would generate in our news media! Every network would cut into its regular programming with bulletins from Jerusalem, and CNN would produce an entire documentary before the sun went down!

Headlines, spotlights, and center stage are addictive. A cynical politician once claimed that leadership was simply finding a parade and getting in front of it. He didn't care what the cause was as long as he got to be at the front of the line and make the speeches. The Gatlin Brothers' song, "All the Gold in California," contains an interesting comment about the psychic cost of hungering for parades: "Living in the spotlight can kill a man outright," notes the line. Our need for the parade can be deadly.

That kind of self-service was exactly what Jesus was resisting in all of these temptations. Jesus chose to be the Savior of the world instead of merely the sensation of Jerusalem.[13] The parade can be extremely risky to the soul. Hunger for headlines and prominence can erode values. One television preacher proudly told me that he was required by his producer to remove his large diamond ring because the glint from the TV lights on the ring was distracting viewers. Another TV preacher smugly noted that he preached to 1.3 million viewers each week and received letters in which viewers claimed to worship him. Neither of these preachers seemed to sense that parades are seductive. The only parades Jesus ever fronted led to a trial and cross.

Luke 4 instructs us in focused ministry strategy. We see Jesus refusing to base his ministry on the strategies of pleasure, power, and parade. Instead, he chose to launch the focus of his ministry, the kingdom of God, by the service principle. Jesus lived out Joseph Campbell's contention that the quest of heroic leaders is "the wisdom and power to serve others."[14]

The Strategy of Service

Jesus declared his service strategy in the Nazareth manifesto. Taking his text from Isaiah 61 to address his hometown synagogue, Jesus read:

"The Spirit of the Lord is upon me,
because he has anointed me
to bring good news to the poor.
He has sent me to proclaim release to the captives
and recovery of sight to the blind,
to let the oppressed go free,
to proclaim the year of the Lord's favor." (Luke 4:18-19)

Then, Jesus proceeded to preach his first sermon, totaling nine words: "Today this scripture has been fulfilled in your hearing" (Luke 4:21).

After announcing his ministry strategy of service to the kingdom of God, he immediately launched into teaching and healing. The general populace, other than his skeptical hometown acquaintances, wanted him to settle down in their territory and establish God's kingdom on their doorsteps. But, always clear about who he was and about the scope of what he was called to do, Jesus repeated his vision and his strategy of service: "I must proclaim the good news of the kingdom of God to the other cities also; for I was sent for this purpose" (Luke 4:43). To us God's kingdom may sometimes seem mysterious, to Jesus it was his mission. It was the rule by which he actually lived his life. Even more relevant to us, the kingdom is the rule he expects us to live by every day. The ministry focus of Jesus is to be our ministry focus too.

Dis-advantages, or Strategic Warnings

What can we learn about the dark side of leadership strategy from Jesus' temptations? Since strategy deals with advantages, the tempting underbelly of strategy deals with dis-advantages. How can we avoid the patterns of "stinkin' thinkin' " in life's tests?[15]

Basically, strategy requires choices—clear, straightforward yes or no decisions. Haziness or sloppiness in thinking, deciding, or acting leads to personal temptations and strategic failures. When we look at what Jesus did and what he didn't do, some warnings about strategy flag our attention.

Strategic Warning #1—Leadership Opportunities: Yes or No? We're most vulnerable when we're on top of the world. Victory—or the prospect of victory—is heady stuff. When ministry opportunities stretch before us, it's tempting to survey the options and to seduce ourselves into believing that we created those open doors ourselves for our own purposes. Sensitive leaders learn to confess excess and ask, "Do these opportunities align with my life's focus?"

Strategic Warning #2—"Exceptional" Leaders: Yes or No? Rarely are we tempted to become world-class scoundrels and to remain gross sinners every day of our lives. Rather, we're more likely to be pointed to the "advantages" of setting aside our vision and values in "this special case." But focused leaders are less apt to deviate from their basic mission.

Strategic Warning #3—Focused from the Beginning: Yes or No? Strategy teacher Michel Robert describes a leader's "driving force"—that unique, singular motive that sets us apart from others and identifies us as different[16]—as foundational for leadership effectiveness. According to Robert, our driving force is the engine that propels our life and work. That engine ought to be cranked up early in our ministries. If our vision and values are not firmly rooted in service to the kingdom of God from the launchpad, the orbits of our ministries may be thrown off course early and, without an accurate compass, never put back on a true course.

Strategic Warning #4—Cheap Grace:[17] Yes or No? You and I aren't often tempted to fail outright. Instead, we're frequently tempted to achieve—but by using shortcuts. When grace becomes cheap or answers glib or ministry easy, be alert for shortcuts wearing the attractive masks of achievement. Focus may keep us from being diverted to take shortcuts.

Strategic Warning #5—Jesus' Focus Doesn't Apply: Yes or No? Don't assume Jesus' temptations were "back then and there" and no longer apply to us today. Take seriously the cautionary note at the end of those temptations: "When the devil had finished every test, he departed from him until an opportune time" (Luke 4:13). If Jesus was never immune from the appeals of temptation, neither are we.

The adversary is a canny strategist. He bides his time. He waits until our guards are down. He makes spiritual warfare as nonthreatening and as unnoticeable as he can. He subtly offers us attractive shortcuts. "Special circumstances," by the devil's logic, are ready reasons to choose pleasure, power, or parade over service to the kingdom of God. But the devil's shortcuts take us down the seductive road to self-service rather than toward the focus of the kingdom of God.

Struggling to Lose

The classic tug-of-war between the strategies of the devil and Jesus are reflected again in a conversation from a medieval monastery. A novice monk asked a seasoned veteran of the abbey, "After you entered the monastery, did you struggle with the devil?" "No," answered the older monk, "I struggled with God." "With God? How do you hope to win?" inquired the startled novice. The older monk softly replied, "When I struggle with God, I hope to lose."

"When I struggle with God, I hope to lose." Hear the clear sense of priority in the old monk's statement? From a strategic point of view, Christians are called to do very few things. Our ministry focus is to be sharp and completely given over to God. We are called to serve God's kingdom, to resist the tempter, to treat our brothers and sisters with love, and to lose our wills to the will of our Father. These unflinching "yes" or "no" choices flow from our strategic focus, a focus like Jesus, our Master Strategist, developed and practiced. Focus in leadership is the basic strategic watershed for effective ministry.

— 3 —
Learning
Focused Leadership

Effective strategic leaders are focused persons. Fortunately, religious leaders have excellent models in focused leadership. We follow Jesus' admonition to seek God's kingdom first (Matthew 6:33). We follow Paul's example to concentrate on "one thing" (Philippians 3:13). That successful kind of focus in life and leadership isn't automatic, however. Focused leadership requires discipline and effort.

Focus: Beginning to End

Focus is a basic factor in many areas of effectiveness, including athletic success. Have you ever wondered why some of the world's fastest 100-meter sprinters rarely win races against top flight competition? Why do they run so well early in races but lose form late, flail their arms, and almost literally fall across the finish line? Instead of a difference in training techniques or athletic ability, success is more a matter of mental strategy. At least, that's the viewpoint of one of the world's fastest men. He claims that most sprinters plan to run only 95 of 100 meters and then try to lunge the last five meters to the tape. This successful sprinter, in contrast, prepares to race by telling himself that he's running 105 meters instead of the actual 100 meters. Since he readies himself to run completely through the tape rather than almost to it, he holds his form and is still accelerating when he crosses the finish line—usually in the lead. That's focus!

Tuning Out the Static

Jesus was a highly focused leader. He concentrated his life and work on valuing and pursuing the kingdom of God. Focus enables leaders to tune out the static, those disturbing and distracting effects in the leadership environment. Focus keeps the main thing as primary and does first things first.

Seeing God Guiding Our Lives

Some of us make sense of our lives simply by living now and figuring out the *why*'s and *wherefore*'s later. If you're an action-oriented learner about yourself and your leadership possibilities, consider this.

Think of your life as a sacred story, a kind of travelogue of personal experiences. Likely only a few of our life experiences are actual breakthroughs into new levels of focus, self-awareness, and self-direction. But these rare episodes serve ever after as focus shapers, identity clarifiers, and career anchors for us. We tend to carry these special turning point memories around in our heads like little videotaped vignettes whose replays remind us of who we are, where we're going, and why we do what we do.

Because these focusing events don't happen often, reviewing them recements the cornerstones of our identify and recreates crucial opportunities for self-reflection about direction and focus. To illustrate, I'd like to play (from among many) three "videotapes" from my life's private library. Picture these tapes as three focusing points in my pilgrimage.

Identity: The first videotape radically focused my attitude about myself as a person and a professional. I came from a supportive family and had excelled in academics and athletics. With a few exceptions, almost everything I had tried had turned out well. By my late twenties, I was completing a doctorate and had invested lots of energy in accumulating ministerial credentials. I was, however, more ordinary than I ever suspected—a "twentysomething," a firstborn, and a person used to competing and succeeding. But I was about to learn some new lessons about myself when I attended a 1969 training event for religious leaders in Kerrville, Texas, with two ministerial friends.

One hundred twenty participants gathered at a retreat center in the Hill Country to learn a variety of ministry skills; my subgroup of a dozen persons worked specifically on conflict management skills. In our first small group session, we were asked to make a name tag for ourselves, revealing something important about ourselves while using only our first names. We were urged to avoid titles, roles, positions, or credentials. Since I was in the final stage of writing my dissertation, when I was being forced to pore over Turabian's form manual as almost a form of "daily devotional," I took a full sheet of red construction paper and created a name tag that looked like a highly structured, formal outline.

As the early days of this nine-day workshop unfolded, I became acquainted with a bright young Presbyterian pastor from Houston. Ken and I worked well together on several projects and enjoyed each other's company—or so I thought. One day as we were walking to the dining hall, he asked me what I did for a living. Before I could answer, Ken speculated that I was a layperson and a computer programmer. I could tell he was surprised when I announced that I was a minister too. He casually inquired, "Presbyterian?" "No," I replied, "Baptist." Ken stopped dead in his tracks and stared at me in total disbelief. Before he could regain his composure, Ken described in graphic terms the questionable lineage of every Baptist preacher he had ever met! Then, he shook his head sadly, admitted that he had begun to like me, but now he would have to evaluate whether we could be friends. With that dazed benediction, he walked slowly away in a stunned state of disappointment.

Frankly, I was shocked. It wasn't his view of Baptists that unsettled me. After all, I too had met some "interesting" Baptists. But I was staggered by having to prove myself, and I was threatened by the possibility that I might not measure up. I realized in that brief exchange that I had moved in small circles and had traded all my life on my family reputation, my formal roles, my academic credentials, and my athletic abilities. Never had I really had to prove myself to strangers in the open market.

I had been previously accepted on "name, rank, and serial number." I didn't know if people liked me for myself or for something I could do for them. Deep down I suspected people liked me for utilitarian reasons.

The next few days at Mo-Ranch were full of new skill discoveries. All the time, however, I knew that Ken was judging me carefully. He approached me three or four days later and told me, somewhat grudgingly, that I was all right in his book. He guessed that we could be friends. For the first time in my life—at least at a conscious level—someone liked me for myself and not for a title, an achievement, or a ministry done for them. It was a heady experience.

When I returned home, my wife observed a difference in me immediately and asked what was happening in me. I told her that I was "high on air" and then tried to describe how wonderful it felt to be accepted as a person on the basis of only my first name and my willingness to try to contribute constructively to my group of peers. I now knew that people liked me, even when they mistook me for a Presbyterian computer programmer. I didn't have to strive for more and better credentials anymore. I had discovered a new, focusing freedom.

Risk Taking: A second videotape depicts an event that encouraged and focused me to take the risks of professional growth. In September of 1972, my wife and I drove to Emporia, Kansas, to attend a continuing education workshop at Lee Douthit's home. The content of the day centered on script analysis, the idea that our lives are scripted like a play. This concept was based on the then-popular theory of social psychiatry called transactional analysis. I was curious but generally skeptical about the possibility that we could have chosen our life's direction at a very young age. Maybe I had become too comfortable explaining my life as "this is just the way I am." The format of the day was deceptively simple. We completed a three-page questionnaire and interpreted our own information under a trainer who guided the entire group. We were looking for childhood heroes or heroines, someone we were unconsciously patterning our lives on. To my amusement but not to my surprise, the Lone Ranger character emerged from my script questionnaire. As a youngster, I had hurried to do my homework and farm chores every afternoon so that I could listen to the Lone Ranger serial on the radio. That memory was familiar. I even remembered what I liked most about the Lone Ranger— his habits of rescuing others, of taking no credit, and of never shooting anyone ever. And, all of these good deeds were done to the beat of the classical music *William Tell* Overture.

But, as I explored my professional characteristics, I discovered some intriguingly similar features. My best friend was (and is) a Native American who had taken risks for both of us. Suddenly, I recalled that Tonto spied out the land while the Lone Ranger waited passively by the safety and comfort of the campfire. Additionally, the Lone Ranger never stayed around for the *thank you's*.

In my ministry, I realize I too had never stayed around for *thank you's*. Instead, I rode away in a cloud of dust (and imagined my grateful parishioner saying, "Who was that Masked Minister?"). The Lone Ranger, complete with mask, silver bullets, and his faithful Indian companion, lived and worked very conservatively. I had essentially adopted his lifestyle too. So, that day I decided to risk some less conservative behaviors. For one thing, I began staying around for the *thank you's*. For another thing, I started writing.

Still, as one who values personal freedom, I wondered how seriously I should really take this life-scripting business. About ten years later while preparing a seminar presentation, I reviewed my notes from the Emporia workshop. One inquiry in the script questionnaire had asked, "If you could do anything you want, what would you be doing five years from now?" I had written, "Teach in a seminary." Frankly, I figured the odds of me becoming a seminary professor were, in the words of Dizzy Dean, "slim and none." But since I actually was a seminary professor at the time I was reviewing my workshop notes, I checked the date of the workshop: September 7, 1972. Then, out of curiosity, I checked the seminary records for the exact date I had signed the official school covenants: September 7, 1977! Five years to the day! Was the timing scripted exactly? This eerie discovery gave me a greater appreciation for life's larger tapestries. Additionally, I was glad that I'd taken the risks of growing and changing in order to be ready for the next act in my life's drama. Again, focus was added to my life by exploring my script and taking the risks of growth.

Contribution: A third personal vignette reminded me how intangible ministry often is and focused me on a tangible outcome. Have you ever wished for more concreteness in your work? Have you worked hard all day and still wondered at nightfall what exactly you had accomplished? Or, have you wished for some objective evidence that you had changed a person or a circumstance?

To illustrate, the day after George McGovern was defeated for the United States presidency, a reporter went by his Washington home for an interview. The reporter arrived while McGovern was cleaning his swimming pool. Given the large margin by which McGovern had lost the election, the reporter was unsure about how to begin the conversation. Finally the reporter asked, "Which is easier, running for the presidency or cleaning a pool?" McGovern immediately responded, "Cleaning a pool. At the end of the day, you can tell what you've done." Most religious leaders can identify with McGovern's observation, especially when we deal with eternity as a time frame for leadership.

My next-younger brother developed a baffling illness in early 1992. He couldn't shake off a low-grade fever and, consequently, underwent nearly four months of extensive medical testing before he was diagnosed with an early stage of leukemia. A bone marrow transplant was his best chance for survival. Family members were tested for matching marrow profiles. Although I was a prime candidate to provide the marrow, somehow my mind found lots of reasons to assume someone else would be the best match.

On September 16, 1992, my phone was ringing when I arrived home from work. From Colorado my sister-in-law excitedly announced, "We've found a perfect match! You!" It was a uniquely electric moment. I don't ever recall feeling such absolute exhilaration and such stark terror wrapped together in a single moment. But the acute emotions were quickly distracted by the practicalities of the calendar. I had only three weeks to reorient my life and schedule for up to three months at the Fred Hutchinson Cancer Research Center in Seattle.

I had only the sketchiest idea of what my brother, I, and our wives were facing when we arrived on "Pill Hill" in Seattle in early October. I knew he would be prepared for the transplant by using a combination of radiation and chemotherapy to kill off the cancer cells and, in the process, to destroy his immune system. I didn't realize how brutal the treatment process would be before the rescue; I wasn't emotionally ready to watch all of my brother's mucous membranes explode and see him deliberately pushed to the brink of death. On my part, I knew I'd have some marrow extracted from my pelvic bones; I hadn't envisioned two surgeons using long, threaded needles to pierce my pelvis two hundred times to harvest one liter of fresh bone marrow. No one had readied me for the AIDS tests and the pointed questions about my lifestyle; I wanted to settle the issue easily by asserting defensively, "Look, I'm a preacher and have never been involved in any of those practices." I hadn't anticipated the variety of medical tests to guarantee that I wouldn't compromise my brother even more. I hadn't thought about the weight of individual responsibility I would feel for my brother after the preparation process passed the point of no return. The anxieties were numerous and heavy.

I dealt with my uneasiness in part by using a calming, centering technique. When the day of the transplant arrived, I found I was ready. I awakened a couple of hours before the harvesting procedure was scheduled to begin and realized I was surveying the day with a different outlook. I now looked on what I was doing as a donation. And I was eager to give my gift. Nobody would have to take my marrow from me; I'd give it.

What difference did this outlook make that morning in Swedish Hospital in Seattle? I was so relaxed that even the surgical team commented to me about my attitude. The operation took only half the predicted time. I didn't bleed. I woke up clear-headed. The next morning I left the hospital, walking stiffly, and went across the street to visit my brother.

Some people called me courageous for donating bone marrow. Actually, courage has little to do with gifts of love. I had something my brother needed desperately. That one fact dominated the situation. My brother had to have a new immune system to increase his odds of living, and my marrow match offered the best possibility to him. I'm sure that if we had had other choices, neither of us would have volunteered to be in the circumstance we were in. But you play the hand you're dealt in life. From a Christian perspective, you're a steward of what you have; and you learn from the experience of contributing.

Miraculously, in Seattle I had a chance to learn a lot of new lessons about my life. One learning was especially crucial for a person like me who works with intangibles so much of the time. This transplant process afforded one of the best occasions in my life to feel I had made an objective difference in another person's life. That view was also shared by at least one other person. In early December after I had returned to Virginia following the transplant, I received a handwritten note from my brother. His message was summed up in the single sentence: "Thanks for saving my life." I had given a gift. More important, I had made a contribution that changed two lives. That was a focusing experience.

Identity, risk taking, and contribution—God has used these, and other, breakthrough lessons to help me keep my life and leadership focused. What are the pivotal videotapes from your sacred stories? Choose some "videotapes" from your own life and work as reminders of the lessons God has taught you in order to help create strategic focus for you as a leader.

Searching Deliberately for God's Direction

Have you developed or used a personal vision checklist as a direction-finder? Have you intentionally selected a personal focus for your life? Let me pose some matters for you to explore.

Ready? Here are some questions intended to stimulate and clarify your lifelong quest for a more specific sense of personal targeting or life calling. These questions are clues to a pivotal issue in a leader's strategic success: What is your vision, purpose, passion, or vocation?

Don't hurry the process of answering the following inquiries. Rather, plant these clue issues as seeds in your mind, and allow them to germinate in their own season. In other words, relax and let these questions "soak." Squelch any built-in impulse on your part to decide these matters for all time—right now—so that you can rush on to another list of things to complete. Vision matures on its own schedule.

Give yourself the luxury of some time to think and, noting your responses on a tablet, see where your detective work takes you:

- Who are my models and mentors? Whom do I admire?
- Which biblical character(s) do I wish to "be like"?
- What are my spiritual gifts? My natural talents?
- When have I grown the most as a person? A leader?
- What have been my primary successes and fulfillments in life? What did I learn?
- When have I failed most painfully? What did I learn?
- When do I feel most motivated and alive?
- When do I withdraw and resist?
- Do I work best alone or in an interpersonal community?
- What kind of people do I enjoy the most?
- What type of work setting or organizational culture do I appreciate most?
- Which habits, blind spots, or negative self-talk undercut my progress the most?
- What values, beliefs, or purposes do I hope to live out?
- If there were absolutely no limits on me, what would I choose to do?
- When have I known myself most candidly?
- What traumas have redirected me?
- Has an event stirred me so deeply that it caused me to vow to take action? What touches me?

• Whose love for me and belief in me has given me roots? Wings?

Your answers to the questions above and to others like them supply you with some clues to your life's direction. Many of these clues are hidden within our histories and ourselves. Some clues are people; others are places and experiences. Sleuthing for your own life vision is one of the most exciting detective stories you'll ever "read"—or write.

By the way, sometimes the quest for God's will is sensed by others first. Nearly a century ago, a young school teacher who was deeply involved in the ministry of his church attended an ordination service. To his surprise, it was his ordination. When he protested, the congregation spoke with one voice, "We see the gifts of ministry in you. We interpret those gifts as a call to ministry. We're ready to set you aside for pastoral service." And, they did. The young teacher, George Truett, led First Baptist Church of Dallas, Texas, to become a congregation of significance and served with integrity and distinction in that church for almost a half century until the 1940s.

Using Targeting Techniques

Focused leaders adopt and adapt a variety of techniques to target their energy on their vision. They recognize their spiritual gifts and become good stewards of their strengths. They clarify their values. Left-brain dominant leaders thrive on prioritizing activities and making "to do" lists. Leaders who emphasize the right-brain hemisphere are more likely to anticipate cycles and build some spontaneity into their worlds.

Whichever brain hemisphere you favor, a personal mission statement is a favorite approach to finding and keeping the main thing as the main thing. The focused personal mission statement provides a clear target and a motivational tone for leaders. Why? Because good mission statements are short and to the point, set a positive

45

and upbeat tone, contain emotionally charged words, reflect daily action, and involve self and others.

Recently, in a leadership development seminar called "Getting in Control of Your Ministry," I updated my personal and professional mission statement. As I reflected on my life and work, an image popped into my imagination—a potter's wheel with clay waiting to be shaped. Holding that mental picture in the background and incorporating the basic Christian virtues of faith, hope, and love in my draft, I wrote the following mission statement to focus and guide my life and work:

I
WILL MOLD
CHRISTIAN LEADERS
through the
joy of training,
thrill of writing, and
fun of conceptualizing ideas
—by living and leading
faithfully at work,
lovingly at home, and
hopefully in my wider world.

Of course, my mission statement is only one sample. But, if you are willing to use one of several resources for crafting a personal mission statement—such as Stephen Covey's *The Seven Habits of Highly Effective People*—you may find new direction for your leadership efforts.[1] These statements have the advantage of providing a big-picture definition for your life and of lending a steadying lodestar against the buffeting winds of the day-to-day demands on our lives and work.

Helping Congregations Find Uniqueness

Leaders help congregations target the "why" of their existence. "Why" gives meaning to organizations. "Why," when augmented by "what" and "where," provides the impetus to help congregations discover and act on their uniqueness.

On many occasions, secular organizations model the way for churches in sharpening institutional directions. A supermarket chain in my city prints its mission statement on its grocery bags: People and food are our commitment. Recently, I saw the mission statement of Microsoft, the gigantic Seattle-based computer software developer: "We envision a computer on every desk and in every home—running Microsoft software." Corporate mission statements—like personal mission statements—serve as compasses for organizations of all kinds.

Hints for Life Focus

Finding focus in life and ministry isn't necessarily automatic. Here are some initiatives leaders can take to find or hone their sense of direction:

- Work constantly at self-definition.
- Retreat, as needed, to sharpen your sense of direction.
- Update your personal mission statement at the beginning of every year.
- Simplify your life by reducing distractions and demands, where possible.
- Surround yourself with friends who will tell you the truth about your blind spots, liabilities, and weaknesses.
- Participate in a spiritual gift discovery process.
- Research your family history in order to understand your own roots and traditions more completely.
- Learn to say "no" to fragmenting opportunities and temptations.
- Explore your sense of calling and vocation.
- When you're affirmed, ask, "What do others see as strengths in me?"

Focusing on the kingdom of God helped Jesus act strategically. Narrowly targeting our leadership efforts is a strategic stewardship of our energies.

47

FLEXIBILITY

The Strategic
Stewardship of
Opportunity

— 4 —
Acts
Flexible Leadership
for Strategic Change

Occasionally, our world experiences a cultural earthquake that shakes our assumptions about the way things are. When these seismic shudders occur, our playing field and all the rules of the game change. These changes can be radical.

Imagine yourself playing tennis. Visualize the court, net, rackets, tennis ball, and your opponent. Now, blink your eyes and consider this confusing scene. You're suddenly playing tennis on an ice rink. Your opponents are eleven fully uniformed football players, the rules are for baseball, and the ball is for golf. Can you take it in? The way you've understood tennis and the way you've behaved as a tennis player will be changed so thoroughly that you'll probably lose decisively and may even give up the game in frustration!

New Paradigms Demand Flexibility

These fundamental alterations of the way we see our world are called "paradigm shifts." When basic paradigms shift, two monumental changes unfold—our boundaries move and our behaviors adjust too.[1] We're suddenly on a new playing field with a different set of rules.

Take the field of medicine as one example of paradigm shifts. A number of historic discoveries have radically changed the ways medicine has been practiced throughout history, shifting boundaries and altering behaviors. Ancient physicians had

51

thought that blood ebbed and flowed through the human body like the ocean's tides; then, in the early 1600s William Harvey discovered that the heart pumped blood through the body and the entire anatomical paradigm shifted. "Evil spirits" and "invisible seeds" were blamed for illnesses until the late 1600s when Leeuwenhoek first saw germs through his microscope and set the stage for Pasteur's research in the 1800s on disease prevention through sterilization. Again the disease paradigm shifted. No longer was it necessary to "bite the bullet" when surgery became more common and humane after anesthesia was made safe for controlling pain in operations during the late 1800s. So the surgical paradigm shifted. Vaccinations, miracle drugs, life-support machines, the wellness movement, and laser surgeries have all continued to revolutionize the art and science of healing. Treatment paradigms have shifted amazingly throughout medicine's history. But medicine is only one example of the fluidity of paradigms.

Jesus as Paradigm Shifter

Religion has seen radical paradigm shifts too. Jesus made the religious world unstable and topsy-turvy; his followers completed the job by turning the world upside down (Acts 17:6). Jesus changed the world's boundaries and behaviors with his works and words. The Sermon on the Mount displays Jesus' paradigm shift. To the Jews for whom the Law was paramount, Jesus took a radical stance. He contrasted what they had heard from their earliest history with "but I say to you" (Matthew 5:21-48). He refused simply to settle for external and technical compliance with the Decalogue. Rather, Jesus, the outsider who knew the old paradigm but refused to be shackled by it, challenged his followers to practice an internalized covenant written on their hearts (Jeremiah 31:33). He changed the rules!

Typical of those rare leaders we call paradigm shifters,[2] Jesus was only partially understood by his sympathizers and was mostly rejected by his critics. In the face of the difficulty others had in grasping Jesus' new paradigm, it's no wonder Jesus called on persons to let their eyes really see and their ears really hear. When paradigms shift, our filters on reality blind, deafen, and deceive us, making new perspectives difficult to accept and flexibility tough to practice.

Acts' Leaders as Paradigm Pioneers

Jesus shifted the religious paradigm, but the leaders in Acts served the Christian movement as paradigm pioneers.[3] Paradigm shifters like Jesus shake their worlds; they function as catalysts, founders, and change agents. But the changes the paradigm shifters trigger are accepted, accelerated, and fully implemented by paradigm pioneers like Luke, Stephen, Philip, Barnabas, Paul, Silas, and other lesser-known leaders in the early churches of Acts.

Paradigm pioneers are intuitive leaders who act flexibly before all the evidence is in hand. Consequently, paradigm pioneers adopt new paradigms with their hearts even more than their heads. According to Thomas Kuhn, expert on scientific revolutions, decisions to practice a fresh paradigm "can only be made on faith."[4] That pattern certainly fits the leaders of Acts.

The flexible leadership of pioneering faith is the stuff of Acts and the early churches. In reality, the book of Acts dramatically presents a paradigm shift launched earlier by Jesus. Paradigm pioneers play by the new rules set by the paradigm shifter. And the new rules require new strategies in order to fully live out changes.

From a strategic point of view, the leaders of Acts and the early churches faced a straightforward but demanding task: how could they respond flexibly to the myriad of new ministry opportunities offered by the Holy Spirit without losing the focus of Jesus? Theologically, they solved the flexibility-with-focus challenge by asserting that the Holy Spirit was implementing the work Jesus had begun in the flesh. Change, consequently, became a mission opportunity rather than a ministry threat.

The Tensions of Transition

Change is tension filled. When paradigms shift, the old and new collide. Typically, new paradigms emerge before the old ones have completely run their course. Consequently, the leaders of the old ways have gained their positions by the mastery of the existing patterns. They, therefore, resist giving up what has worked and still continues to work to a degree. Besides, the leaders of the new paradigm have no track record to cite yet. There are no guarantees amid change. So living betweentimes is tough. We all prefer to live by the mountain climbers' motto: don't turn loose of what you have before you have a firm grip on something new.

Most of us become rather traditional amid transitions. We naturally lean on our routines and ruts. Paradigm expert Joel Barker makes an important distinction for strategists. Barker notes that you and I manage within a paradigm but we lead between paradigms.[5] Managers deal with routine and the "what is" of stable organizations and cultures; leaders deal with risk and the "what can be" of worlds in transition. For Barker, a leader is "a person you will follow to a place you wouldn't go by yourself."[6] Leaders serve as tour guides for adventures many aren't ready to risk.

Several years ago, Wes Seeliger distinguished between two kinds of theology: settler and pioneer.[7] Using images from the opening of the American West, Seeliger contrasted an increasingly domesticated religion of the settlers with a wilder, freer faith practiced by pioneers. Settler theology prefers the places and routines of town life over the discomforts of the wagon train. Settler churches are like town halls where the citizens enjoy a sedate Sunday morning tea party. All is pleasant and predictable. Until. Until, as Seeliger views pioneer theology, this radically unpredictable cowpoke—we would call the Holy Spirit—rides madly through the town shooting up the tea party at the city hall and generally upsetting the citizens. Settlers find their paradigms pinched by the conflicts so typical of new frontiers. Frontiers and transitions require paradigm pioneers who can take risks.

54

When Acts is read as a case study in flexible leadership strategy amid rapid change, the book makes mystics of us all. Page by page paradigm shifts unfold, and the missionary movement of early Christianity marches into new frontiers of ministry. Of course, the Holy Spirit is the real paradigm pioneer who pushes back the barriers and interrupts the traditional tea parties in order to inaugurate the mission explosion we know as early Christianity.

Structures and Strategies in Acts

Dr. Luke has left a valuable legacy to the students of leadership strategy. Luke's perspective documents the entrepreneurial leadership of Christianity's missionary expansion. He follows the pilgrimage of the new faith from Jesus' birth to Paul's imprisonment, chronicling the middle third or so of the first century. As the sole Gentile author and the writer of a two-volume biography and history in the New Testament, Luke's saga recounts the victors and victories in early Christianity. Luke was certain that Jesus Christ was the Savior of all people of all kinds everywhere.

Luke described two generations of missionary activity. His global Gospel recorded "all that Jesus did and taught" (Acts 1:1). Acts ends by noting that Paul proclaimed "the kingdom of God and [taught] about the Lord Jesus Christ . . . without hindrance" (Acts 28:31). But Acts is more than a description of the work of Paul and the other apostles and more than a missionary travelogue about how Rome was eventually evangelized. Acts is the story of how the gospel was freed and how it expanded its impact on the world in the face of seemingly insurmountable hurdles. Acts tells us that Jesus started something that can't and won't be stopped no matter what the barriers are. Those different obstacles also show us how different ministry strategies were applied flexibly to different challenges to the Christian gospel.[8]

The book of Acts is structured around six panels of an estimated five years each.[9] Each panel concludes with a progress report on the expansion of early Christianity. Like a televised documentary presented in miniseries format, the Christian victors and victories in the six episodes of Acts picture the unhindered momentum of missions in spite of major barriers. The drama is intense as the gospel triumphs in spite of persecution and conflict (Acts 1:1–6:7), cultural differences (Acts 6:8–9:31), physical, racial, and political barriers (Acts 9:32–12:25), geopolitical challenges (Acts 12:25–16:5), jealousy and argument (Acts 16:6–19:20), and subversion and human bondage (Acts 19:21–28:31). From a flexible leadership viewpoint, each of the panels demonstrates a distinctive, entrepreneurial, proactive missionary strategy. Strategic focus is pursued flexibly and aggressively.

Strategy Changes—Panel by Panel

Marketers observe that services and products have life cycles.[10] Over time, the same message must be presented by different methods in order to maintain its appeal to current sympathizers or to expand its appeal to different groups. Otherwise, the message begins to lose some of its edge. This pattern of strategic adjustment unfolds as the work of the Holy Spirit expands in Acts from panel to panel.

The six panels depict six different mission expansion strategies. These missionary strategies vary from empowering to diversifying to anticipating to launching to expanding to planning—each applied flexibly as new challenges are met and mastered. The tides of change are evident in the implied questions underlying each panel of Luke's Volume II, the Acts.

Empowering Strategies (Acts 1:1–6:7)

When Luke's Volume I closes, Christianity is tightly linked to Judaism. The existing paradigm for ministry shifts when empowerment strategies are triggered by Pentecost. So the first panel of Acts raises the question: How did the gospel move beyond Judaism? The answers to that pivotal question vary, but each answer nudges Christianity beyond the Jewish synagogues. The gospel moved beyond Judaism by witnessing to the ends of the earth (Acts 1:8), by depending on the Holy Spirit's empowerment (Acts 2–3), by withstanding persecution (Acts 4, 5:17-42), and by dealing effectively with dissension (Acts 4:36–5:16; 6:1-6).

Empowerment strategies strengthen leaders for the risks they face. Where does the power for mission and ministry come from? Acts, sometimes called the Gospel of the Holy Spirit,[11] demonstrates strongly that power is God's gift through God's Spirit to believers. The Holy Spirit is obviously the high profile actor in Acts with more than forty references to the Spirit in the first thirteen chapters of the book alone. The theme of the Holy Spirit as empowerer appears in the very first paragraph of Acts: "you will receive power when the Holy Spirit has come upon you; and you will be my witnesses" (Acts 1:8). This theme echoes again in Acts 4:31 when "they were all filled with the Holy Spirit and spoke the word of God with boldness."

Pentecost (Acts 2 and 3) is the prototypical empowering episode in the New Testament. Acts 2:4 states the case succinctly: "All of them were filled with the Holy Spirit." Four major entrepreneurial actions flowed directly out of this empowering event. (1) Immediately, the believing community witnessed to God-fearers from a variety of language groups (Acts 2:5-12). (2) Then, Simon Peter preached persuasively about a purposive God and his redemptive work through Jesus Christ—so persuasively that three thousand persons accepted the Christian lifestyle (Acts 2:14-41). (3) The church assimilated the new believers, sharing so unselfishly and praying so fervently that still others joined them (Acts 2:42-47). (4) Public healing grew out of the ministry of Peter and John. The empowering work of the Holy Spirit is shown dramatically in Acts' first panel.

A motivational speaker reports a story about a woman who, out of 1200 salespersons, led her company in sales and broke every industry record. When asked how she did it, she replied, "God didn't make me with an off-switch!" Maybe the Holy Spirit takes away our off-switches and turns on our power as leaders.

The empowerment strategy panel concludes: "The word of God continued to spread; the number of the disciples increased greatly in Jerusalem, and a great many of the priests became obedient to the faith" (Acts 6:7). The Holy Spirit's power revolutionized believers' lives.

Diversifying Strategies (Acts 6:8–9:31)

The second panel of Acts shows another paradigm shift in Christian missionary growth: How did the gospel reach out to the Grecian Jews? The answers to that question provide us some important clues to mission strategy. Evangelism occurred by steadfast witness (Acts 6:8–8:40), by converting enemies (Acts 9:1-19*a*), and by preaching to the unconverted (Acts 9:19*b*-30).

Diversification strategies use a variety of approaches, flexibly increasing the odds of success and lowering the risks of defeat. This panel—especially as seen in the ministries of Stephen and Philip—demonstrates a range of attitudes and initiatives that extend the gospel's influence. Stephen, the first believer to see Christianity in a worldwide perspective, presented words and works that offended the Jews. When they argued with Stephen, however, they found they "could not withstand the wisdom and the Spirit with which he spoke" (Acts 6:10). By beginning a new era of missionary expansion when he pointed out that God had never limited himself to one land or one temple (Acts 6:11–8:1), Stephen opened a new door of witness. This message, unfortunately, cost Stephen his life. But, if the blood of the martyrs is the seed of the church, the same gospel Stephen had preached was sown by Philip in the new fields of Samaria and Ethiopia (Acts 8:4-13 and 8:26-40). In the case of both of these pioneering missionaries, the Christian message was proclaimed to increasingly diverse audiences.

Acts' second panel sums up the progress resulting from the use of diversification strategies: "Meanwhile the church throughout Judea, Galilee, and Samaria had peace and was built up. Living in the fear of the Lord and in the comfort of the Holy Spirit, it increased in numbers" (Acts 9:31). Empowerment and diversification were obviously an effective first-line combination of mission strategies.

Anticipating Strategies (Acts 9:32–12:25)

Acts' third panel raises another question about the progressive march of the Christian faith: How did the gospel reach the Gentiles? The answers are radically straightforward. The flame of the good news spread by re-examining attitudes (Acts 9:32–11:18), by means of some pioneering outreach (Acts 11:19-30), and by standing firm in the face of official pressure (Acts 12:1-23).

Anticipation strategies allow leaders to deal well with what's expected and to take corrective actions early, or better yet, in advance of problems. Anticipation strategies also help us cope better with the unexpected. A pivotal episode in anticipation strategy occurred in Acts 10 when Peter envisioned that with God there are no clean or unclean animals. But, it took two additional reruns of the vision before Peter realized that God loves all of his human creatures too. Finally, he was able to assert: "God shows no partiality, but in every nation anyone who fears him and does what is right is acceptable to him" (Acts 10:34-35). Slow as he was to see the scope of God's love, Peter soon told his experience with conviction to the Christians in Jerusalem. Their response expanded their horizons for the gospel. "When they heard this, they were silenced. And they praised God, saying, 'Then God has given even to the Gentiles the repentance that leads to life' " (Acts 11:18).

Bud Wilkinson, legendary head football coach at the University of Oklahoma, died in February of 1994. His sports legacy reflects anticipation strategies.[12] Wilkinson's record speaks for itself. He led Oklahoma teams to three national championships, engineered an incredible forty-seven game winning streak, and coached thirty-two All-American players. Wilkinson innovated the split-T formation, the no-huddle offense, and organized practice schedules. What was the secret to his success? How did Oklahoma under Wilkinson regularly beat bigger and faster teams? Preparation. J. D. Roberts, one of Wilkinson's All-

Americans, notes, "An Oklahoma football team under Bud Wilkinson was never unprepared." When Wilkinson was honored in the late 1980s with the Amos Alonzo Stagg Award, he echoed Roberts' observation: "If you have the will to prepare, things will usually work out quite well, and the will to win will take care of itself." Wilkinson practiced the strategies of anticipation.

Women in Christian ministry know much about this strategy of anticipation, especially when they are juggling the demands of professional ministry with the often unequal burdens that are theirs for raising children or keeping the household intact. The woman who is summoned unexpectedly by the school to pick up a sick child, is prepared for the many unexpected crises, such as death or illness, that appear to disrupt the plans of a congregation.

Anticipation strategies practice flexibility and pay dividends. As this panel's summary report notes, "the word of God continued to advance and gain adherents" (Acts 12:24).

Launching Strategies (Acts 12:25–16:5)

The fourth panel in Acts deals with the issue of "How did the gospel become aggressively missionary?" Again, the strategies are obvious. Christianity spread by appointing missionaries (Acts 12:25–13:3), by appealing to persons who already had some religious sensitivity (Acts 13:4-43; 14:1-7), by turning to pagan audiences (Acts 13:44-52; 14:8-20*a*), by stabilizing new churches as they were established (Acts 14:20*b*-28; 15:36-41), and by freeing dynamic faith from organized religion (Acts 15). Launching strategies enable us to start new initiatives with vigor.

The fourth panel records two bold acts of launch-oriented entrepreneurial strategy: the first Christian missionaries were appointed, and they shared the gospel with pagan audiences. Paul and Barnabas were set aside for mission service (Acts 13:3). The early efforts of this team were still aimed toward traditional groups. When their message was rejected, however, they deliberately offered the Christian message to persons in Lystra who had no Jewish background (Acts 13:46-51 and 14:8-20*a*). It's almost as if these pioneering missionaries foresaw Bear Bryant's philosophy. The legendary coach kept a sign in his team's locker room with a simple challenge typical of launchers: "Cause something to happen!" Another launch practice is noted when Paul and Silas revisited churches in Syria and Cilicia to stabilize and instruct them. This panel's progress report notes these launches and subsequently announces, "So the churches were strengthened in the faith and increased in numbers daily" (Acts 16:5).

Expanding Strategies (Acts 16:6–19:20)

The fifth panel inquires, "How did the gospel move beyond the Jews?" Christianity expanded aggressively by evangelizing the West (Acts 16:6-10), by using many methods for one message (Acts 6:11–18:23), by updating followers' faith (Acts 18:24–19:7), and by insisting on basics (Acts 19:8-20).

Expansion strategies increase the range of possibilities by extending horizons and making ministry more comprehensive. Panel five records a dramatic geopolitical expansion of Christianity. What had been an Eastern religion now moved purposefully to become a Western faith too. When Paul's troop accepted the invitation of the Macedonian man to "Come over to Macedonia and help us" (Acts 16:9), the missionary enterprise entered a radically new phase of expansion. The paradigm changed again under flexible leadership. The world became Christianity's mission field, and the gospel was freely preached on "foreign fields." Suddenly, citizens of major centers like Philippi, named for the father of Alexander the Great, and Thessalonica, named after Alexander's half-sister, were hearing and believing the gospel of Jesus Christ.

When the gospel moved West, changes happened rapidly. Paul and the early Christian strategists must have noted a strange phenomenon. Their world was moving so fast that the doubters who had been saying the missionary work couldn't be done were suddenly being interrupted by pioneering women and men who were already expanding missionary ministry.

This panel on expansion strategies ends with the observation, "So the word of the Lord grew mightily and prevailed" (Acts 19:20). Luke's vision of a global gospel was becoming a reality.

Planning Strategies (Acts 19:21–28:31)

The issue of the sixth panel is "How did the gospel 'travel' to Rome also?" Mission work in Rome resulted from sticking to the long-range plan (Acts 19:21–20:38), from contending successfully with zealots (Acts 21:1-26), from risking self-exclusion (Acts 21:27–23:10; 28:17-28), from facing bureaucracy (Acts 23:11–26:32), and from witnessing to the end (Acts 27:1–28:16).

Planning strategies focus on purposive advances and on efforts "to write history before it happens." The hopes of Paul and the purposes of God unfold in the final panel. The twin goals of Jerusalem and Rome are on the horizon—both reflecting how the Jews and Gentiles responded to the Christian gospel. It's important to remind ourselves again that the gospel, not Paul, is the star of the drama in Acts. It's the missionary advance of Christianity under the Holy Spirit that's featured here.

The ancient mariners held a superstition that inevitably one wave comes along that is greater than anything that has preceded it. They called it the Ninth Wave. Somehow the sea and wind teamed up to create this unique force. The seafarers further believed only those who planned carefully and timed their actions were able to catch the Ninth Wave's crest and ride it.

When the Ninth Wave—the wave we call Christianity—gained its missionary momentum, only flexible planner-strategists could keep up with the pace and scope of expansion. The gospel had been freed to be preached in Jerusalem and Rome and beyond. There was no stopping the gospel's progress.

When Paul finally arrived in Rome, he called the Jewish leaders together. The closing paragraph of Acts describes the relentless forward march of the Christian movement. "From morning until evening he explained the matter to them, testifying to the kingdom of God and trying to convince them about Jesus both from the law of Moses and from the prophets. Some were convinced by what he had said, while others refused to believe. So they disagreed with each other; and as they were leaving, Paul made one further statement: 'The Holy Spirit was right. . . . this people's heart has grown dull, . . . this salvation of God has been sent to the Gentiles; they will listen' " (Acts 28:23-28). From a leadership strategy viewpoint, Acts tells us the gospel always belongs to the flexible and the faithful.

When the subtitles roll on the missionary miniseries we call Acts, the concluding progress report sums up what the paradigm pioneers, led by Paul, had accomplished under the Spirit's power. He "welcomed all who came to him, proclaiming the kingdom of God and teaching about the Lord Jesus Christ with all boldness and without hindrance" (Acts 28:30-31).

Strategies for Flexible Leaders

The strategies of Acts' six panels challenge us to practice flexibility in leadership. However, the required elasticity may not be as overwhelming as it appears at first. The six panels of Acts, when viewed from a flexible leadership perspective, show a spiral of three clusters of strategic behaviors repeated twice. Each of these behavior sets identify leaders with special aspects of flexibility. For example, empowering and launching strategies call for start-up artists, those rare leaders who can get a new enterprise off the ground. Diversifying and expanding strategies feature entrepreneurial actors, those leaders who can tolerate high risks comfortably and set the pace without becoming frozen. Anticipating and planning strategies call for future-oriented adventurers whose eyes are always fixed on the horizon. These male and female leaders in Acts and the early churches were remarkably flexible and creative.

Leadership for a New Order

Paradigm shifts require leaders who can implement that challenging trinity of results, resources, and risks with focus. The leaders in Acts set the pace by applying flexible strategies to the opportunities the Holy Spirit offered them. That's a lesson for us too. In our day, the whole world has become a mission field. In fact, we are called to become "missionary pastors."[13]

But applying missionary strategies is difficult. Because change is accepted slowly, the early Christian leaders of Acts are especially to be admired and imitated. Consider this reaction to a paradigm shift from another era. Aristotle was considered the greatest thinker of his day, and he believed the conventional wisdom: the heavier the object, the faster it would fall to earth. For nearly two thousand years Aristotle's belief prevailed. Then, in 1589, Galileo summoned a group of distinguished professors to observe an experiment. He gathered them at the base of the Leaning Tower of Pisa, went to the top, and simultaneously dropped the equivalent of ten-pound and one-pound weights. Both hit the ground at the same time. Guess what happened. The power of the old paradigm was so strong, the professors denied what they'd seen. Refusing to believe their eyes, they remained blinded by their paradigm.

Maybe Machiavelli had it right: "There is nothing more difficult to take in hand, more perilous to conduct, or more uncertain in its success than to take the lead in the introduction of a new order of things." Thank God for the paradigm pioneers who, without sacrificing the ministry focus of Jesus, risked flexible leadership on the missionary frontiers described in the book of Acts!

ACTS AS MISSION STRATEGY:

Examining the Panels of Acts for Strategy Pointers

EMPOWERING STRATEGIES
(Acts 1:1–6:7)

Begin where you are geographically (1:1-8)
Rely on God's Spirit (1:9–2:13)

Acts: Flexible Leadership for Strategic Change

Preach what you know (2:14-47)
Use resistance to toughen resolve (3:1–5:42)
Organize for ministry (6:1-7)

DIVERSIFYING STRATEGIES
(Acts 6:8–9:31)

Count the cost of bold missions (6:8–8:3)
Let the gospel confront your prejudices (8:4-40)
Enlist leaders for future work (9:1-31)

ANTICIPATING STRATEGIES
(Acts 9:32–12:25)

Recognize new fields of service (9:32–11:18)
Avoid a superstar attitude (11:19-26)
Allow adversity to build fellowship (11:27–12:25)

LAUNCHING STRATEGIES
(Acts 13:1–16:5)

Use base camps as launch pads (13:1-3)
Appeal to the half-converts (13:4-41)
Respond to the responsive groups (13:42–14:28)
Declare doctrine clearly (15:1-35)
Stabilize new believers (15:36–16:5)

EXPANDING STRATEGIES
(Acts 16:6–19:20)

Take advantage of new openings (16:6-10)
Visit strategic sites, win groups, and train them for mission
    (16:11–19:20)
Communicate in the audience's thought forms (17:16-34)

65

PLANNING STRATEGIES
(Acts 19:21–28:31)

Set a goal and act on it (19:21–21:26)
Exercise persistence (21:27–28:16)
Endure rejection for a free gospel (28:17-31)

— 5 —
Adapting
To Flexible Leadership

"Seize the day!" That was the advice of the Roman poet Horace (65–8 B.C.) when he exclaimed, "*Carpe diem!*" Horace saw a stark truth: When opportunity knocks, flexible leaders are ready and able to take the risks of striding boldly across the threshold into a new day. When the faint knock of a ministry paradigm shift is heard, two options emerge: The new day must either be entered and seized now or forfeited and lost forever. In a pivotal situation when there's a new day to be seized, flexible leaders—like those in Acts—make the difference.

A Credo for Flexible Leaders: "Spirit Surfing"[1]

How were the leaders in Acts so deftly able to sense and so readily able to respond to the ministry opportunities created by the Holy Spirit? Strictly from a leadership perspective, they demonstrate an unusual gift for juggling two crucial factors in strategic success—focus and flexibility. Rarely are leaders able to maintain a sharp focus while also responding creatively to new opportunities. Too often, modern strategists become either inflexibly focused or flexibly unfocused. But the leaders in Acts were strategically ambidextrous, equally adept at both focus and flexibility. Consequently, Acts' leaders were able to keep the old faith and still seize the new day. That's an example for us to follow now.

Focus with flexibility is a difficult balancing act. A Garth Brooks song, "The River," describes life's dream as a moving, changing, surprising river. The river's flow forces the navigator to remain flexible within the focus of life's vision. Some navigators drift along without seizing the day and must be challenged to "choose to chance the rapids and dare to dance the tide."[2] Those exceptional leaders who can manage to stay in the mainstream of the visionary river and still dare to dance the tide are strategically effective.

Moving to Deeper Levels

Political cartoonist Pat Oliphant has offered an interesting clue to the pursuit of flexibility. Oliphant draws a political cartoon every day. To keep his idea hopper full, he reads widely and constantly for ideas and images. When an idea for a cartoon pops up, Oliphant doesn't settle for too little. He assumes an idea that emerges easily is likely an idea that other cartoonists or editorialists have also thought of. How does he, then, deal with the possibility that others have had the same or at least a similar idea too?

Oliphant takes his basic idea and then moves it to a deeper level. By pushing the concept into a different and richer framework, he opens the option of new insights or truths—and, hopefully, of humor. Of course, moving beyond the obvious into the new and untried is a risky step, but this risk may lead to breakthrough discoveries.

Risks Are for Taking

No one—especially religious leaders—can live flexibly without taking risks. Of all persons, religious leaders should recognize that risk and faith are near-synonyms. For religious leaders—in Acts and now—risks are for taking. Why? Because they are expressions of personal faith.

Breakthroughs usually grow out of significant risks. Do you know about the risks taken when *South Pacific* was written and staged? In 1944, when James Michener was approaching forty, he was in the Navy and stationed on a remote South Pacific island. To fill his time, he began writing short stories about the region. Although advised that short stories were difficult to get published, Michener took the risk and persisted. His book received good reviews, and, more impressively, won the Pulitzer Prize.

After the book was introduced to composers Richard Rodgers and Oscar Hammerstein, they crafted a musical from Michener's story. Then another risk was taken when the movie version was cast. A middle-aged opera singer named Ezio Pinza was given the romantic lead. The book and musical make up a saga of risk taking. As a result of a series of strategic risks, *South Pacific* has become a popular book and a beloved musical. Playing it too safe blocks us from significant contributions and stimulating adventures.

Riskers: Made or Born

Why do members of the same family choose to live their lives differently? Why do some siblings take big risks, while another brother or sister seems content to play life close to the vest? Some observers of human nature claim some of us are natural riskers or entrepreneurs, but others of us are more cautious by nature. Some of us push life along; others wait for life to push us. Some of us can more easily take strategic risks; others resist risks, strategic or not.

My grandfather grew up in a family of eight, but unlike his siblings, he ventured far away from the family home. As a teenager in the late-nineteenth century, Granddad worked in a Virginia coal mine. One day a runaway coal car came careening down its tracks and trapped my granddad in a narrow underground passage. His head was pressed against the wall of the passage by a sharp corner of the coal car. As Granddad described it, the car's corner functioned like a can opener; it turned his head 180 degrees and peeled the scalp away from the skull. While his scalp was being sewn back on, Granddad made a strategic decision—he decided the mines were no place for him! Acting strategically, he left Virginia and his family behind, went to Ohio and built some of the first telephone lines, and then took an even bigger risk of moving to the frontier of western Kansas to homestead a wheat farm. Granddad had an entrepreneurial bent, a perspective fitting to the frontier, but his other siblings apparently didn't share or exercise that same entrepreneurial outlook and stayed behind.

Some leaders are apparently born with the gift of flexibility—like entrepreneurs. Other leaders—like most of us—must develop the plasticity of their personalities. Which kind of leader are you? How will you expand your leadership flexibility?

Think Like an Entrepreneur

We've long heard of intense, driven type A and relaxed, laid-back type B personalities. Recent research suggests a third cluster of behaviors classified type T for thrill seekers. T's search out challenges and accept them. Skydiving, bungee jumping, and risky stunts are the desserts in type T's banquet of life. I wonder if there's also a type E, a natural-born entrepreneurial personality. I see theological E's throughout the book of Acts.

Acts brims with entrepreneurs, those naturally flexible riskers. And why not? It was their special time in Christian history, one of those expansionistic betweentimes eras when the new and different become the standard operating procedures for believers.

Between paradigms, entrepreneurs excel. Entrepreneurs are leaders who undertake new and risky ventures with energy and initiative. They have a passion for results, a sense that all failures are temporary, and the will to keep on keeping on. While bureaucrats settle for operating existing organizations, entrepreneurs push back the frontiers and build for the future.

Entrepreneurial women and men have the ability to stay focused on a few key strategies, but they pursue their goals flexibly. (1) They find a need and meet it. Filling vacuums and satisfying unmet needs are almost sure roads to success. (2) They know the new is attractive. "New" is one of the most powerful words in an entrepreneurial leader's vocabulary. (3) They recognize that success occurs when preparation and opportunity meet. Entrepreneurs don't rely on luck. They get ready to be effective. (4) They know what they really want in life—in case they get it. No real leader wants to be like the dog who chased cars, caught one, and then didn't know what to do with it. (5) They determine in advance the limits of sacrifice. They know when to "hold 'em" and when to "fold 'em." Entrepreneurs have a keen sense of when to cut their losses and move on.

Entrepreneurialism has an unfortunate dark side, however. Entrepreneurs march to the beat of their own drummer—and may even compose their own music. The independent risk taking that helps entrepreneurs succeed can also sabotage them. Entrepreneurs often don't work well as subordinates or staffers. They generally aren't gifted in developing others. They may function well when organizations are new and small but may remain too "hands-on" when the organization outgrows their style. They sometimes try to motivate by reward or fear. They can be so driven to achieve that they are menaces to themselves and others. They may resist others' ideas and become stubborn and unbending. Entrepreneurs may be angry and impatient. Steve Jobs, founder of Apple Computers, was eventually fired by his board for his unbending attitude.[3]

In Acts the leaders were clearly entrepreneurial. Happily, they avoided most of the menacing underbelly of the entrepreneurial bent by staying focused and flexible.

Act Like an Intrepreneur

The book of Acts and the new congregations reflected by the epistles of the New Testament hint at a subtle strategic change in leadership. Because entrepreneurs basically think like outsiders, a new breed of paradigm shifter began to emerge—the intrepreneur. Intrepreneurs were change agents who worked inside organizations comfortably. They were gifted leaders who kindled an innovative spirit in existing organizations and viewed themselves as agriculturists—plowing, planting, cultivating, and praying for rain. Intrepreneurs combined dissatisfaction with patience and frequently found success.

From a strategy viewpoint, intrepreneurs—then and now—hold and act on a few basic beliefs. (1) They believe the best decisions are made nearest the work. They lead "by walking around" and stay in touch with the grass roots. (2) They know the most effective communication is face to face. Intrepreneurs ask, listen, hear, and respond to information from those who are on the front lines. (3) They are convinced that innovation is basic to organizational health. Every idea or service or organization finally becomes obsolete, so intrepreneurs are always looking for the next need to meet and the next person to serve. (4) Intrepreneurs know that volunteers work better than draftees. They lead by coaching rather than dictating. (5) Intrepreneurs use an improvement cycle. They determine what "it" is—and focus on "it." Then they create, test, fix, and offer "it." (6) Some leaders settle for a "trial and error" approach to life. Intrepreneurs believe in "trial and success." Because they take lots of risks, they make lots of mistakes—and learn from them. Learning from our mistakes is a vital element of effective leadership. (7) Intrepreneurs think *small, others,* and *now.* Inside organizations, change may happen slowly. Attempting incremental change for others when the opportunity presents itself adds up to significant change over time.

Fifteen Steps to Flexibility

What can you and I do if we weren't born entrepreneurs or intrepreneurs? How can we cultivate more flexibility in our lives and leadership? The suggestions listed below are ways people like us have used to stretch their imaginations and challenge their assumptions about what God is doing in the world.

Read widely, including at least one out-of-the-ordinary
    title or topic each month.
Travel to a place you've never visited before.
Ask open-ended questions.

Listen more than you talk.
Break an old habit.
Try a new food.
Converse (not argue) with someone who looks at life
    differently than you.
When you fail, try again—from a different angle.
Cultivate a new hobby.
Become expert on a foreign country.
Take novel routes to familiar destinations.
Make "what if" a frequent phrase in your vocabulary.
Play games, and laugh at surprises.
Go to a creativity workshop, and experiment with
    alternate solutions.
Read the book of Acts annually.

Ten Acts-ions of Flexible Leaders

The flexible leaders of Acts teach us several powerful lessons about the faith of paradigm pioneers. Ten "Acts-ions" reflect the dynamics of faith and change in the book of Acts.

The First Acts-ion: Have enough faith to fail. Faith is never a "sure thing." The only persons who never fail are those who never attempt anything. Riskers—and "faith-ers"—don't play it safe. Pioneers live on the edge of the frontier. Consequently, they fail consistently but temporarily. Ultimately, leaders' faith doesn't expand by trial and error. If we learn from our stumbles, we quickly learn to operate by trial and success. In Acts, even persecution became an occasion for enlarged vision and strategic ministry.

The Second Acts-ion: Move beyond rehearsal and take the "show on the road." Faith adopts a "take charge" stance toward life. We follow a God on the go, a God who prefers tents to temples, and is always a step ahead of us, blazing trails, and beckoning us to catch up. God was moving fast in the Acts' record and was calling for the church to hurry up and join in the sweep of redemption.

The Third Acts-ion: Interpret change. Change loses some of its fearsomeness when leaders frame and contextualize transitions. In Acts, pacesetters regularly identified God at work in new ministry opportunities. Frequently, the eyes of faith saw the continuity of God's patterns of redemptive activity in situations that, to the faithless and inflexible, appeared to be stark breaks with all that had come before.

The Fourth Acts-ion: Ask, "What if?" and "Why not?" Faith holds a possible/positive view of the future. The Holy Spirit guided the leaders in Acts to expect great new opportunities from God; those leaders then attempted great things for God.

The Fifth Acts-ion: Find folks who "do faith" well and emulate them. Faith follows faith and builds its own momentum. Models, mentors, and mates show us the way. Faith makes friends; faith takes friends. After all, Christianity is a communal religion. Leaders are shepherds of the flock, not just of individual sheep. Paul and Barnabas stand out as leaders who befriended, encouraged, and sponsored others as the early faith community launched out on increasingly riskier ventures of ministry and missions.

The Sixth Acts-ion: Tolerate ambiguity. Faith does not demand certainty or expect life without anxiety. I asked a sailor friend how he felt the first time he sailed out of sight of land. He answered, "I wasn't afraid. But I was mighty glad to find that distant island where it was supposed to be!" Faith leaves the shore behind and accepts the uncertainty of being beyond eye shot of what has been left and of what's being sought. Leaders in Acts were almost always on the high seas of missionary expansion.

The Seventh Acts-ion: Expect to be disoriented by change. Change is upsetting; it spins our heads around. New challenges and novelty throw all of us off stride and erode our self-confidence. Though left uncomfortable, leaders face the disequilibrium of change squarely. Faith accepts the discombobulations of new endeavors as a matter of course. The pace of change in Acts was so drastic that it's a real lesson in the stabilizing power of faith when the leaders of the early church kept their heads and their ministry focus.

The Eighth Acts-ion: Prepare to be changed by the Holy Spirit. Faith—especially when it's new, fresh, and mushrooming—affects our lives dramatically. New, emotional experiences can radicalize us. They give us momentum; they propel us toward untested attitudes and into untried behaviors. C. S. Lewis points out that conversion is deep transformation, not merely shallow improvement.[4] Believers in Acts lived with open minds, hearts, and hands. They remained curious and inquisitive.

The Ninth Acts-ion: Focus on the advantages of change. A review of our personal and professional growth spurts reminds us that life's most difficult times often become extremely fulfilling. Faith sees change as a catalyst for growth. The leaders of Acts testify to faith's equation—that change equals growth—on both individual and congregational levels.

The Tenth Acts-ion: Cultivate a holy unrest. Faith is, by definition, adventurous. The faith-full leader believes that, "If it ain't broke, break it!" After all, history is only made by discontented persons. In Acts, lots of history was made because the Holy Spirit refused to allow believers to fall into an easy pattern of comfort. They never assumed they had arrived.

Develop "Opportunity Eyes"

Jesus repeatedly challenged his followers to develop eyes that really see. The ability to see opportunities, break old mind-sets, and sense new paradigms emerging is basic for flexible leaders. Cultivating curiosity for new information from a variety of sources, sensing trends early, and acting proactively opens our "opportunity eyes." I prefer the instinctive strategy of hockey star Wayne Gretzky: "I skate to where the puck is going to be, not where it was."

Seize the Day!

Strategic leaders are targeted leaders. They have a sharp focus in life and ministry. They know where they're going.

75

However, when new ministry options emerge, focus can lock into the old, blind us to possibilities, and cause us to ignore paradigm shifts. The leaders of Acts modeled focus—but with flexibility. The lesson is clear but challenging: when the Holy Spirit gives a door of fresh ministry to us, seize the day!

FUTURE - ORIENTATION

The Strategic Stewardship of Horizons

— 6 —
Pastoral Epistles
Future-Orientation for
Congregational Strategy

Leadership is always situation-specific. Different ministry circumstances tilt us toward different leadership strategies. For instance, as congregational life began to emerge in the New Testament, local church ministries became a natural focus of the strategy efforts of the fledgling churches. Like most contemporary congregations, few New Testament era ministers or churches could be "all things" to all persons (1 Corinthians 9:22). So they concentrated on consolidating their ministries around their local needs and solidifying their home bases.

Consolidation of congregations emerged as one evident concern in early Christianity. The New Testament's letters to the churches often revolve around answers to specific, localized questions.

The trend is apparent. Once missionary work had succeeded in establishing a church in a given setting, significant effort shifted toward stabilizing and cultivating the ministries of that new church. That's the nature of organized life. When institutions emerge, the focus tends to shift rather quickly from the movers and the movement to the machine and its monuments. There's an obvious built-in warning for traditional churches in that historic trend: established institutions often pour their best energies into maintenance, and they lose some of their passion for mission— unless they deliberately commit themselves to health, vitality, and the future.

The potential threat to established organizations becomes a strategic reality when they begin to act like the establishment. Establishment churches concentrate on hanging on instead of building on. Instead of serving, they preserve and conserve.

Roots or Wings?

In the New Testament, one of the sections in which the energies of the movers and the movement tilts noticeably toward machines and monuments is in the popularly titled "Pastoral Epistles" to Timothy and Titus. The more "establishment" viewpoint of the Pastoral Letters provides a striking contrast to the more "entrepreneurial" perspective of the book of Acts. In terms of leadership strategy metaphors, the tension here is between roots and wings. The Pastoral Epistles emphasize roots more and argue: "Churches put down our roots so that we may spread our wings, if we choose." Acts, on the other hand, had stressed wings more and challenged: "Why not fly and stretch our roots by the action?"

The tension between roots and wings is contemporary as well as historic. For example, social psychologists can document that most Americans prefer a sanctuary-based religion over an arena-oriented faith. Modern Christians are more likely to withdraw from the world than introduce our world to the kingdom of God. In other words, you and I minister in a culture where congregants generally value roots more than wings.

Offensive and Defensive Strategies

Acts and the Pastorals reflect noticeably different leadership strategies and "time zones." Acts shows Christians on the offensive, taking a focused gospel flexibly to unfamiliar places and new people groups with the future spotlighted. In contrast, the Pastorals are more at home defending the Christian message and past traditions. Listen carefully to the strategic tone and time horizon of the Pastorals.

"fight the good fight, holding on to faith . . ." (1 Timothy 1:18-19, NIV).
"Guard the good deposit that was entrusted to you . . ." (2 Timothy 1:14, NIV).
"Endure hardship with us . . ." (2 Timothy 2:3, NIV).
"continue in what you have learned" (2 Timothy 3:14 NIV).
"correct, rebuke, and encourage—with great patience and careful instruction. For the time will come when men will not put up with sound doctrine" (2 Timothy 4:2-3 NIV).
"straighten out what was left unfinished . . ." (Titus 1:5 NIV).
"hold firmly to the trustworthy message as it has been taught . . . encourage others by sound doctrine and refute those who oppose it" (Titus 1:9 NIV).
"rebuke them sharply, so that they will be sound in the faith" (Titus 1:13 NIV).

Our ears tell us the flavor of the Pastorals is more defensive than the tone in the book of Acts. This tone is a clue to altered strategic approaches and past time horizons.

Whether our strategic orientations grow out of artistic pursuits, sports, military, marketing, family systems, or planning, leadership strategy tends to be either offensive or defensive. Note some contrasts. Offensive strategies play well on the road, establish beachheads and explore frontiers, open new territories, produce more new offspring, and plan for the future. Defensive strategies play better on their home courts, tend base camps and build forts, defend old territories, nurture existing members, and solve today's problems.

Is ministry strategy, therefore, a simple "either-or" matter? No. When only offensive approaches are adopted, strategy loses its stabilizing, rooted elements and becomes faddish. "Offense only" strategies are all wings and no roots. The theological left is susceptible to this shortcoming. Or when only defensive methods are used, strategy forfeits its surprising, winged aspects for tightly defined propositions. Defensive strategies in ministry may lead to a reactionary stance typical of the theological right, majoring on "status by negation."[1] "Defense only" strategies are all roots and no wings. But, neither family of strategies by itself provides enough balanced options to remain effective in our complicated and ambiguous world.

81

In fact, most ministry opportunities require a blend of offensive and defensive strategies in order to be successful amid the varied demands of ministry situations. We need the more winged offensive strategies, such as those modeled by Acts, in order to attack our paradigm's perimeters where the outposts of God's kingdom need to be expanded. We need the more rooted defensive strategies, such as those demonstrated by the Pastoral Letters, in order to establish and stabilize the kingdom's base camps. The flexibility, innovation, and entrepreneurial activities of the offensive strategies need the stability of the fixed, traditional, and conserving impulses of the defensive strategies. And defensive strategies need to be challenged and stretched by offensive strategies.

To use military metaphors, the front line needs the fort. Otherwise, the Christian army may be at risk. On the one hand, a dangerous leadership strategy pinch occurs when a "front line mind-set" develops that neglects basic training, issuing supplies, and MASH support. The warrior's lust for adventure becomes addictive and invites rashness. On the other hand, another strategy imbalance happens when the "fort mentality" substitutes for the front line's action. Caution becomes the watchword and opportunities for advance are missed.

During the Civil War, President Lincoln was constantly plagued by commanders who trained troops well and prepared elaborate battle plans—but rarely went to battle. General Grant may have had traits Lincoln didn't particularly admire, but the President described Grant in two words: "He fights." Consequently, Grant's fighting spirit was reason enough for Lincoln to make him the Union's primary field commander. Grant neglected neither the fort nor the front line. That's a mark of an effective strategist.

The Time and Timing of Strategy

The Pastorals depict a strategic watershed related to time and timing: Will we lead toward the future or the past? Established organizations are constantly torn between their old traditions and their new opportunities. Older institutions are tempted to back into the sunset while looking at their world through a rearview mirror. But leaders deal in the future—particularly strategic leaders.

Effective congregational leaders focus flexibly on the future. As they pursue their strategies, they keep three aspects of strategy in mind. (1) They keep focus in their future by zeroing in on a few functions of ministry. (2) They stretch for flexibility by adopting a "two things at once" mentality of ministry. (3) They target a faithful future by enriching the core of centered wholeness in their life and work. The Pastoral Epistles show us the way to the future.

Template of Ministry

The letters to Timothy and Titus have been described as the earliest handbook on congregational ministry, written to give church leaders some direction in how to do their work. When the Pastorals are read with an eye toward congregational ministry strategies, an interesting pattern emerges. That pattern suggests a template to inform, shape, and sharpen a future-orientation for congregational ministry strategy.

Major Functions of Congregational Ministry

Think of pastoral ministry functionally. What exactly do pastoral leaders do? What are the basic, strategic ministries fundamental to local church health and effectiveness? Answers vary, but one functional model of pastoral ministry provides a threefold template: Pastors proclaim, care, and lead.[2] Proclaiming the whole gospel, caring for the whole person, and leading the whole church, then, are bedrock functions of congregational ministry. Each congregation, with the help of its pastoral ministry team, must cover these three bases. Not every minister or lay leader is equally gifted in each of these three functions of ministry. Therefore, one of the fundamental challenges for local congregations who want to seize their future is to discover and develop a balance of skills in proclaiming, caring, and leading—for the kingdom's sake.

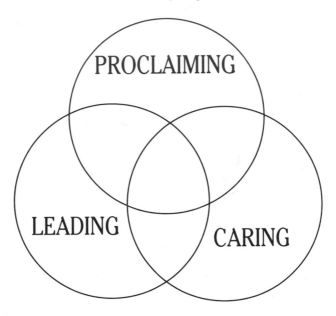

Note that I'm choosing to use gerunds (nouns that are trans-formed from active verbs) for these major strategies. These functional initiatives permeate the leader as a state of being because they are an ongoing pattern in present and future ministry rather than static episodes or isolated actions.

Functions and Strategies

The proclaiming, caring, and leading model helps us explore ministry through an array of pastoral strategy questions that focus the future. What do I do best in ministry? Worst? What does my congregation do best in ministry? Worst? Are my church and I a good strategic match? Where do my church and I need to grow as a ministry team? What training is needed in order for lay leaders, for any other staff ministers, and for me to help our congregation minister in a healthy, balanced fashion? What does this model suggest about the historic view of ministry in my faith family? About the curriculum of my seminary? How well prepared am I to function in ministry? The functional model of congregational ministry—identified above—matches the pattern in the Pastoral Epistles. Note the pattern in the abridged, *Readers' Digest* version of the pastoral letters outlined below.

The First Pastor's Handbooks—
1 & 2 Timothy & Titus

Friends Timothy & Titus,
I wish I could join you and serve with you personally. Since I can't visit you now, I'm sending you a handbook for ministry (1 Tim. 3:14-15). You are clear on what kind of person a pastor is to be (1 Tim. 3:1-7 & Titus 1:6-9). Now here's what a pastor is to do—a kind of pastor's job description.
Prayerfully, Brother Paul

Strategy: PROCLAIMING the Whole Gospel

Study, preach, teach, and witness to the Bible's teaching with urgency (1 Tim. 4:13; 2 Tim. 2:15 & 4:2-5).
Confront bad religion with strong teaching and personal faith (1 Tim. 1:3-20; Titus 1:5-16).
Never be selective when you pray for or witness to God's creatures (1 Tim. 2:1-8).
Be willing to pay the price for faithful proclamation (2 Tim. 3-12).
Let your life and faith be a public and private example (1 Tim. 3:1-7 & 4:12; 2 Tim. 2:22; Titus 1:6-9).

Strategy: CARING for the Whole Person

Give constructive care to the bereaved (1 Tim. 5:3-5).
Supply mutual support for personal needs (1 Tim. 5:3-5, 16).
Encourage fellow pastors (1 Tim. 5:17-25).
Guide troublemakers toward truth and greedy persons toward

stewardship (1 Tim. 6:3-21; Titus 3:9-11).
Love and minister to persons out of the gifts God has given you
(1 Tim. 4:14-15; 2 Tim. 1:6-7, 14 & 2:1).

Strategy : LEADING the Whole Church

Practice the Golden Rule in all relationships (1 Tim. 5:1-2).
Meet destructive attitudes with positive actions (2 Tim. 2:23-26;
1 Tim. 4:7-8).
Help the congregation select godly, growing leaders (1 Tim.
3:8-13; Titus 2:1–3:8).
Respect the service of women in the church (1 Tim. 2:9-15 & 3:11
& 5:9-15; Titus 2:3-5).
Aid persons to become good stewards of their lives, work, and
possessions (1 Tim. 6:1-19).

Congregational Strategy 101: Doing First Things First

Our ministry template pictures a generalist's approach to strategic leadership. Although the ministry model features overlapping and integrated functions, these three functions can be examined separately before they are related as a whole.

Proclaiming the Whole Gospel

Proclamation is defined broadly in our functional model. To proclaim the gospel, we preach, teach, evangelize, worship, do missions, and model the good news of Jesus Christ by the way we live. These skills are prominent in the New Testament's list of spiritual gifts, are emphasized in seminaries and training schools, and are demanded by congregations.

The Pastoral Epistles stress the critical nature of good proclamation. Heresy was threatening the infant church.

The pastor is clearly instructed to "have a firm grasp of the word that is trustworthy in accordance with the teaching . . . to preach with sound doctrine and to refute those who contradict it" (Titus 1:9). The hucksters and deceivers had to be confronted, and new believers had to be carefully nurtured. There was no substitute for sturdy proclamation, in the view of the Pastorals.

Historically, proclamation skills were among the earliest of the pastoral skills to be taught to Christian ministers. These arts and crafts have been developed mainly for settings of one to many. But preaching and the other proclamation efforts are frequently customized now for a wide range of demographic groupings and special interests. Some congregations tailor their worship experiences by focusing them for different constituent groups. For example, they may have a traditional worship service for mainstream audiences, a celebrational worship experience for contemporary-oriented seeker groups, and an instructional service for discipling old and new believers.

Caring for the Whole Church

The Pastoral Epistles also emphasize the care of souls. The life circumstances of older men and younger men, older and younger women, widows, slaves, and the difficulties of youth are all highlighted in the Pastorals as requiring the wisdom of careful guidance. Encouraging others is a frequent exhortation in the Pastorals.

To care for persons in the community of faith and beyond, we counsel, listen, and encourage one-on-one as well as through networks and in support groups. Some pastoral care needs are so pervasive they receive priority emphasis. For instance, because families are changing rapidly and because loss is central to human experience, many congregations offer an array of family enrichment ministries and grief recovery experiences. Pastoral care as a clinical discipline has emerged over the past half century with the development of psychology as a legitimate science and through the rise of the clinical pastoral education movement. In the past, care skills have been slanted mostly toward one-on-one situations and remedial care. More recently, however, family systems research and systems theory in general have broadened our caregiving perspectives considerably and have challenged us to provide better preventive care.

Leading the Whole Congregation

The third functional ministry area of leadership gets its due in the Pastoral Epistles too. Selecting able and credible leaders is strongly emphasized. Lifestyle, reputation and record, a wholesome family life, and a pattern of personal holiness are basic qualities the Pastorals target in leaders for the early church (1 Timothy 3:1-13 and Titus 1:6-9).

In comparison with the pastoral skills of proclamation and care, pastoral leadership is the new kid on the theological studies' block. Only the last two decades have seen much concentrated effort on deepening and enlarging the leadership perspectives of ministers. Increasingly, the one to a few settings of committees, boards, and councils are seen as the make-or-break watersheds in ministry effectiveness. Leadership is rapidly becoming an important skill that's taught in theological curricula and valued in congregational life.

Major Strategies and Meta-strategies

Let's draw a distinction between two kinds of strategies—major strategies and meta-strategies. Major strategies are highly visible and focus on keeping the main things the main things. In the functional model of pastoral ministry, the three actions of proclaiming, caring, and leading are major strategies.

But, this functional model has some subtler aspects, some meta-strategies. "Meta" usually means "behind" or "beyond" or "after." Meta-strategies, then, point us toward the strategies behind, beyond, or after the major strategies. In the functional model of congregational ministry, meta-strategies are the advantages or edges we discover in the overlapping areas of the model.

Meta-strategy 101:
Doing Two Things at the Same Time

The double overlap areas of the model open the door for the application of meta-strategies. Three overlaps—proclaiming and caring, caring and leading, and leading and proclaiming—allow ministry strategists to do two things at the same time. Intentionally looking at ministry in overlapping terms allows us to be better stewards of our ministry opportunities and to work more efficiently.

When we preach pastorally, we combine proclaiming and caring. When we intervene to enhance congregational health, we combine caring and leading. When we articulate congregational vision, we combine leading and proclaiming. In all of these cases, we are choosing to apply meta-strategies in ministry. In these instances, congregational leaders are meta-strategists and good stewards of horizons who are intentionally doing two kinds of ministry simultaneously.

Meta-strategy 102: Nurturing the Core

The triple overlap area in the center of the model calls attention to the core of ministry and reminds us to nurture the heart of our ministry as an intentional ministry strategy. I believe the model's center moves beyond the mere "doing" of ministry's functions to the "being" of the minister. The convergence of ministry's functions in the center of the model pictures centered wholeness. We are called to nurture our spirits and grow toward wholeness through the riches of Christ before we offer to minister to others in his name.

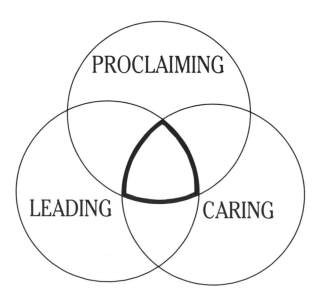

The Pastorals strongly affirm that the person who tries to be true to Christ will be undergirded by that same Christ. For example, 2 Timothy 2:11-13 presents us with a hymn fragment or a few lines of an early creed to remind us of the trustworthiness of the Christ who saves and glorifies us:

> If we have died with him, we will also live with him;
> if we endure, we will also reign with him;
> if we deny him, he will also deny us;
> if we are faithless, he remains faithful—
> for he cannot deny himself.

Our integrity as leader-ministers flows out of the covenant constancy of Jesus Christ rather than from our own cleverness or adeptness.

Unfortunately, integrity or centered wholeness is frequently lacking in contemporary ministry, charges Eugene Peterson. He observes:

> The pastors of America have metamorphosed into a company of shopkeepers, and the shops they keep are churches. They are preoccupied with shopkeeper's concerns—how to keep the customers happy, how to lure customers away from competitors down the street, how to package the goods so that the customers will lay out more money.
>
> Some of them are very good shopkeepers. They attract a lot of customers, pull in great sums of money, develop splendid reputations. Yet it is still shopkeeping; religious shopkeeping, to be sure, but shopkeeping all the same.[3]

It is this stance and style of shortsighted ministry that's described graphically by Flannery O'Connor as being one part minister and three parts masseuse.[4] From an ethical perspective, leadership expert Warren Bennis warns leaders not to cut their consciences to fit this year's fashions.[5] The point is stark: there's no integrity in cheap ministry.

Where, then, is the hope of wholeness? Peterson's prescription or antidote for a shallow, success-oriented approach to ministry lies in the nurture of the minister's spirit through prayer, Bible study, and providing spiritual direction to others. In other words, only a rich relationship with God keeps pastors oriented toward the highest and most powerful Source of grounding.

The Compass of Integrity

Leaders are forced to make tough choices daily. In the face of difficult decisions, our choices reveal our values. Decisions are like the Rorschach inkblot test for leaders, displaying our values by the choices we make. If decisions mirror our core values, then the anchor that integrity provides for leaders is vital.

Contemporary leadership theorists agree that it is crucial for leaders to nurture their integrity, seen as centered wholeness or coherence.[6] They see a leader's integrity as providing an internal compass or a gyroscope. Listen to their comments about integrity from their interviews with business leaders:

> Outstanding leaders have sources of inner direction . . . a compass, set by important life experiences, that guides leaders through the daily pushes and pulls of . . . work. . . . Values coupled with a competitive vision provided a powerful compass that enabled these leaders to keep . . . on strategic course, to differentiate important issues from unimportant ones, and to evaluate more readily potential second-order consequences— the ripple effect—of their actions.[7]

This quest for integrity in who we are and what we do is a pilgrimage most of us continue until the end of our lives. It stands at the center of what we do as ministers in the triple overlap of our model.

What Makes Us Distinctive?

By nature, templates are fixed implements. They help us give shape to things—in this case, our pastoral ministries. Our congregational ministry model has helped us look at our work from a fixed perspective. But, if we are to minister strategically, we have to assume a more dynamic stance and question our outlook.

From a strategic point of view, there are some questions we can ask about our ministries to lessen the chance that we'll become too "establishment," too defensive, too traditional, or too neglectful of our integrity. Let's conclude our consideration of congregational strategy with a practical application to your own ministry.

Think of your work's future strategically. **What makes your work distinctive?** In comparison to other persons or groups, what's unique about the ministries and services you offer to the audiences you touch?

Here are some strategy questions for you to use to look for potential distinctives in your ministry. These strategies apply especially to settled congregations and other established service organizations.

"FIRST"?—What services can you deliver first and faster than anyone else? Do you beat others to the punch? How can you improve the speed with which you respond to needs and requests?

"BEST"?—What services do you offer that are best? What ministries do you provide that are truly excellent and simply better than anything else that's available? How are you actively evaluating our ongoing work? How are you searching for enhanced quality in all of your services and materials?

"NEW"?—What services do you provide which are new and on the cutting edge of innovation? When are you anticipating emerging needs? Where is your ministry "state of the art"? How are you building "research and development" into the fabric of your regular work? How are you listening to success stories, experimenting with possibilities, and conducting pilot programs in order to develop new resources?

"NOW"?—What services do you offer that are so "now" and so flexible you can seize the moment and respond with exquisite timing? When do you strike while the iron is hot? Are you using technologies to deliver ministry at the drop of a hat?

"WOW"?—What services of yours "wow" and pleasantly surprise your audiences? When do you respond in ways others hadn't anticipated? How can you take the offensive and seize the initiative in areas or with resources that take folks agreeably off-guard?

"FACE"?—What services do you put a face on and personalize better than others? How can you answer phones and correspondence, meet and greet persons, and relate to others in warm, direct, impressive ways—ways that put faces and names with services?

"NEIGHBOR"?—What services do you provide that are neighborly and are obviously geared to the needs, hurts, and wishes of others? How are you discovering the real needs of church members and community inhabitants in order to provide *for them* more fully and sensitively?

"MOST"?—What services and resources do you possess in such quantity that you have the most of these items and enjoy obvious superiority? How are you amassing relevant information, ministry expertise, audience goodwill, and other ministry advantages?

"WHO"?—Whom do you serve? How well do you know the persons and institutions in your community? Which new groups are you reaching out to?

Use your answers to these inquiries to keep a creative, offensive edge on your ministry. Guard against becoming too comfortable in your ministry.

Back to the Future

Established congregations and other ministry institutions have the advantages of stability and heritage. Their strategic disadvantage is the built-in temptation of the establishment to prefer the present and past to the neglect of their future. Strategically, to sacrifice the future is suicide.

— 7 —
Keeping the Future
Our Target

Most of us have felt the powerful tug-of-war between the past and the future. In *Creating a New Civilization*, futurists Alvin and Heidi Toffler graphically describe history as "a succession of rolling waves of change."[1] The Tofflers claim three great waves of change have occurred so far. The agricultural civilization, lasting several thousand years and symbolized by the plow, was the First Wave. Then, the Second Wave, called the Industrial Revolution and characterized by factory smokestacks, swept the agrarian world away. Now, after three hundred years, the Third Wave, depicted by the computer and reflecting an information age, is inundating us.

We experience this tug-of-war acutely for two reasons. (1) History seems to be accelerating—a world with its fast-forward button stuck. Some observers speculate that the Third Wave may last only a couple of decades into the new millennium. (2) Living in a time overlap creates an "intergenerational generation." We're the last generation of an old world and the first generation in an emerging civilization. Both waves are swamping us simultaneously. Yesterday is ebbing; tomorrow is building into a tide.

Eyes on the Horizon

Tomorrow is what leaders long for and dream about. We trade in tomorrows, futures, and horizons. Unfortunately, when we become The Establishment, we may lose our attention to the future and begin to become preoccupied with the past. If *status quo* and tradition become our prime values, they make poor guidelines for leadership. The organizational protectionism of a tradition-rich past tempted the leaders in the Pastorals too, a temptation that can prove fatal.

Avoiding the Temptations of Tradition

Traditions and routines can serve us well—as long as the ministry paradigm of our era doesn't change. But, when the whole ball game changes, the old playbook no longer serves the team well. New ministry situations remind us that the varied temptations of tradition may become dangerous to the future.

(1) The "past is best" temptation crops up when religion becomes nostalgic. When the past is worshiped, when we yearn for responding to our environment with the same solutions that were preferred by our denominational founders (like Calvin, Luther, Wesley) we aren't apt to learn accurate lessons from the past or to be open to the future. Staying young at heart is a stretch for older leaders.

(2) The "new is bad" temptation arises when we adopt a Luddite approach to the future. The Luddites, named for Leicestershire workman Ned Ludd, were nineteenth-century English workers who destroyed labor-saving machinery as a protest against technology and change. A century ago the British Parliament actually debated whether or not to close England's Patent Office; some leaders argued that everything had already been invented. We act like Ludd's offspring when we take the attitude that everything worthwhile has already been done.

(3) The "here is good" temptation grows out of a narrow, parochial perspective. When ideas are rejected because they apparently grew in another denomination or a different culture's garden, we have fallen into the "elsewhere is bad" trap. Jonah was so blinded by his view of the Ninevites that he couldn't offer them God's message or believe that they could be forgiven. Narrow parochialism blinds leaders and followers to the possibilities of the future.

(4) The "it's already known" temptation asserts itself when we arrogantly assume we know everything already. That outlook, of course, blocks us from becoming lifelong learners. One of the

prime challenges for leaders of established institutions is staying teachable and "green above the ears." Eric Hoffer observed, "In times of change, learners inherit the earth, while the learned find themselves beautifully equipped to deal with a world that no longer exists." The times are always changing—and so must we, if we hope to be pacesetters in congregations.

Institutional Leadership: a Love/Hate Relationship?

In changing times, how can leaders appreciate institutions without loving bureaucracy? It's a tough balancing act, isn't it? We need organizations to lend mass and stability to our dreams. We enjoy the teamship of coworkers who share the same calling and work toward the same goals on a day-to-day basis. So, institutional life has its advantages. The pinch occurs, however, when size, tradition, and partnership become ends in themselves. When organizations subtly cease serving people and begin to use people, an institution has become a bureaucracy.[2] In practical terms, when we sell our souls to "the company," we become bureaucrats. Metaphorically, we may also become "clock makers."

A clock is an apt metaphor for bureaucracy. Bureaucrats count on living in a predictable universe. They want a world with simple, routine problems and a stable, moderate rate of change. Bureaucrats appreciate precision, regularity, and an even pace of activity—just like a clock.

To create organizational predictability and tidy processes, bureaucrats structure clocklike organizations. (1) Bureaucrats prefer hierarchies with pyramidal chains of command. They want to know who's in charge—and who isn't. Tick-tock. (2) Bureaucrats expect vertical communication channels. They separate the "brains" of the upper echelons from the "hands" of the lower ranks. Bureaucrats visualize leaders at the top of the heap knowing all and telling the followers at the lower levels of the organization what to do and when to do it. The few order around the many. It's the "code of the West"—organizationally. Tick-tock. (3) Bureaucrats divide labor into specialties.

97

They assume specialists are more valuable to organizations than generalists. Tick-tock. (4) Bureaucrats admire technical competence. Technical credentials determine advancement. Tick-tock. (5) Bureaucrats assume an impersonal relationship between leaders and followers. Impersonal power allows for compliance to be coerced if necessary. Tick-tock. (6) Above all, bureaucrats insist that a rule can be crafted to deal with every contingency. "It's in the policy manual." Tick-tock. (7) As a result of the six aspects of bureaucratic behavior noted above, bureaucracies become top-heavy and self-protective. Tick-tock, tick-tock.

When these attitudes are entrenched, persons—including leaders—begin to love and protect their bureaucracies rather than simply appreciating the advantages of their institutions. Their goal in life becomes keeping the bureaucracies intact and in good repair.

You Might Be a Bureaucrat If . . . [3]

Bureaucrats tend to be cautious, traditional, institutional loyalists. They operate by habit, are rule-bound, and become highly dependent on authority and the comforts of organizational life. Are you ready to test your own attitudes about organizational life? Do you admire the traits noted above? Do you appreciate these qualities in your organizational life? If "yes" is your answer, then you might be a bureaucrat.

You might be a bureaucrat if . . . your favorite devotional reading is a policy manual.

You might be a bureaucrat if . . . you are offended by anything "new and improved."

You might be a bureaucrat if . . . you only feel really at home when you're inside the womb of an organization.

You might be a bureaucrat if . . . you automatically say "yes, sir" to everyone—men, women, children, and statues.

You might be a bureaucrat if . . . your supervisor wore a bow tie yesterday and—just to be safe—you wear one today.

You might be a bureaucrat if . . . you believe the boss never, ever makes mistakes.

You might be a bureaucrat if . . . your superior consigns you to hell and, without a question, you simply requisition an asbestos suit and march into the fire.

Organizational Pharisees

Bureaucrats function as the Pharisees of modern organizations. Rule-enforcers, strict, narrow, blindly loyal—and proud of these traits—depicts the pharisaic outlook of bureaucrats. At their extreme, bureaucrats become pathological. A pathological bureaucrat is "one who inverts ends and means."[4] Then, they insist on the letter of the law rather than the spirit of the organization's vision, go by the book instead of moving toward the organization's goals, and protect the status quo in contrast to renewing the organization's future. Parallel to the Pharisees of the New Testament, pathological bureaucrats are stricter, more rigid, and more arrogant about their uncompromising and unyielding stance than anyone else in the organization.

Kaleidoscopic Organizations

Clocklike institutions aren't apt to serve changing or chaotic circumstances well. Clocks don't work when the pace is uneven; clocks don't cope well with novel problems. In those situations, predictability is gone, and clocks are worthless. Clocks can measure yesterday and today. In contrast, tomorrow baffles clocks and bureaucracies. Instead, the future calls for kaleidoscope-like organizations. Kaleidoscopes provide multiple reflections of their world. The scenes are always shifting inside kaleidoscopes. Somehow changing landscapes feels like a more accurate picture of our universe. In our historical era, leaders have to learn to "thrive on chaos."[5]

Kaleidoscopic leaders operate on nonbureaucratic beliefs. Kaleidoscopic leaders believe in the future: bureaucrats defend the past. Kaleidoscopic leaders believe that organizational direction grows out of vision, trust, teamwork, and cooperation; bureaucrats count on authority and control to prevent change. Kaleidoscopic leaders believe organizations must renew, change, and grow; bureaucrats assume defensively that they have somehow already arrived. Kaleidoscopic leaders believe organizations function best when members feel secure, supported, and appreciated; bureaucrats prefer for members to depend on them—even if pressuring and tyrannizing members is the only way to remain in authority. The leadership contrasts in kaleidoscopic and clocklike organizations are stark and clear. Those contrasts are frequently the difference between the past and the future.

Keeping the Future Before Us

What kind of things can leaders do to stay young above the ears and to keep an eye on the horizon? Spend time with children who have much more future than past. Play. Continue to learn. Believe in miracles. Go on an adventure. Ask God to surprise you. Create something new. Watch a novel manufacturing process. Visit a site that's strange to you. Read something on a topic that's completely foreign to you. Surf the Internet.

A deadly way to become set in our ways and forget to scan horizons is to focus on the past. Roger von Oech's *A Whack on the Side of the Head*[6] identifies ten "mental locks" that tie us too closely to what we think we already know. (1) "The Right Answer," (2) "That's Not Logical," (3) "Follow the Rules," (4) "Be Practical," (5) "Avoid Ambiguity," (6) "To Err Is Wrong," (7) "Play Is Frivolous," (8) "That's Not My Area," (9) "Don't Be Foolish," and (10) "I'm Not Creative" are assumptions or attitudes that limit our odds of seizing a new future. Any one of these approaches narrows our options of discovering fresh new strategies for fresh new days. Taken together, these mental locks are fatal to strategic leaders.

Hindsight Versus Foresight

Leaders of established organizations frequently find their options narrowed by the history and position of the institutions they have created. They need to recover their range of choices rather than having their course chosen for them. "The things of God are full of foresight," observed Marcus Aurelius. Is it true, then, that the thoughts of bureaucrats are filled with hindsight? The Establishment may work so hard to preserve and protect its past that it often overlooks the possibilities of the future. Strategic leaders refuse to forfeit their future.

FEASIBILITY

The Strategic
Stewardship of Crisis

— 8 —
Revelation
When Survival
Becomes the Agenda

Historian Barbara Tuchman has paid a high compliment to Enguerrand de Coucy, a fourteenth-century French nobleman. In noting his death, Tuchman describes de Coucy in an unforgettable phrase: "He was a whole man in a broken time." What an epitaph! A whole man in a broken time!

Fourteenth-century Europe had more than its share of brokenness—the Black Plague, the Hundred Years' War, invasions of the Ottoman Turks, peasants' revolts, and the division of the Catholic Church under rival popes. In the face of such fragmentation, de Coucy wasn't shattered by adversity and didn't forfeit his values. It's a victory of character and strategy to remain whole when your world is breaking apart. And that's exactly the challenge first-century Christians faced when the book of Revelation was written while their time in history was turning the corner into the second century.

Wholeness Amid Brokenness

Revelation was a whole book for a broken time. An apocalypse or an "unveiling," the only book of its kind in the New Testament, Revelation was written to offer encouragement during an extreme situation. The book is truly a tract for tough times. Written from a concentration camp and crafted in the code of colorful words and mysterious images, Revelation's format is more akin to riddles, allegories, song lyrics, numerology, and cartoon pictures than straightforward newspaper prose. Speaking to desperate circumstances, the book announces hope and wholeness powerfully and unforgettably. More than 80 percent of Revelation's paragraphs feature a hortatory tone and outlook, urging and advising confidence in God as well as courage for daily living.

Consider the brokenness of Revelation's era. Religious persecution and banishment were rampant. Despair threatened believers, and some were renouncing the faith. Evil—in the sinister, tandem form of dangerous government and sick religion—was in the driver's seat. Annihilation was a looming possibility. That's brokenness!

But, consider the wholeness of Revelation and its message. Believers were encouraged to stand firm. Comfort was promised, hope was supported, and the faith was assured by Christ's triumph. There was safety in the midst of disaster. Since evil can never overpower God's purpose, believers were challenged to catch the spirit of courage and serve in spite of adversity. That's wholeness!

Revelation still offers a holistic message for broken times. Our own near-end-of-a-century world is broken too. We face war, AIDS and other catastrophic diseases, bigotry, disregard for the value of people, sick religion, and moral confusion. When our dreams and hopes are in jeopardy because of chaos beyond our control, are there still some hopeful possibilities? Revelation answers with a resounding, "Yes!"

Feasibility Strategies in Action

Even when our ultimate future is assured, our current times can still be broken and pressurized. Our day calls for believers to choose carefully and wisely. From a strategic thinking standpoint, when the long view of life is compressed into a minute-by-minute exercise in survival, we tailor our strategies primarily to survive now and then to thrive later. Feasibility strategies identify what's possible now, an especially crucial leadership tactic amid crisis. Crises force us to choose survival strategies when our immediate circumstances seem impossible.

In Revelation, three feasibility strategies are apparent. (1) Survive the crisis with faith intact. (2) Encourage each other with the conviction that God will ultimately triumph. (3) Plan to return to the strategic focus of earlier days and treat the current crisis as a hurdle to be overcome rather than a permanent state of affairs. Feasibility settles for the simple, practical actions that allow us to cope with today and preserve a tomorrow.

Painting the Landscape with a Broom, Believing More Recklessly, Behaving More Playfully

Revelation's vision is from the heart and for the heart. Encouraging believers to live faithfully and optimistically is the core vision of Revelation. Given its upbeat message in tough times, Revelation takes the longer view from a wider angle. The book paints Christian leadership's landscape on a panoramic canvas with a broom. Such a vision requires reckless and playful expression in order to be lived out effectively. Eugene Peterson states Revelation's perspective powerfully and poetically:

> Some, when God is the subject, become extremely cautious, qualifying every statement and defining every term. They attempt to say no more than can be verified in logic. They do not want to be found guilty of talking nonsense. Others, when God is the subject, knowing how easily we drift into pious fantasies, become excessively practical. They turn every truth about God into a moral precept. But poets are extravagant and bold, scorning both the caution of the religious philosopher and the earnestness of the ethical moralist. St. John is a poet, using words to intensify our relationship with God. He is not trying to get us to think more accurately or to train us into better behavior, but to get us to believe more recklessly, behave more playfully—the faith-recklessness and hope-playfulness of children entering into the kingdom of God. He will jar us out of our lethargy, get us to live on the alert, open our eyes to the burning bush and fiery chariots, open our ears to the hard-steel promises and commands of Christ, banish boredom from the gospel, lift up our heads, enlarge our hearts.

St. John sings his songs, represents his visions, arranges the sounds and meanings of his words rhythmically and artistically. He juxtaposes images unexpectedly, and we see and hear what was there all the time if we had only really listened, really looked. He wakes up our minds, rouses our feelings, involves our senses.[1]

Will we confront any built-in cautiousness and false piety in order to tune our ears to God's encouragement? Will we choose to live our lives on larger canvases with more recklessness and playfulness? If we can hear the poet's heart and if his heart speaks to our hearts, then Revelation points the way to wholeness in a broken time.

Dramatic Encouragement Amid Crisis

How should leaders face crises? The crisis setting of Revelation reminds strategists of three basic leadership actions. (1) In crisis, decide to survive. (2) In crisis, encourage your partners in ministry. (3) In crisis, resolve to return to the basic pillars of strategy: focus, flexibility, and future-orientation. Revelation points the way for leaders who choose to live hopefully amid the brokenness of crisis times.

Revelation's Playbill

Revelation has been depicted as a drama with seven acts plus a prologue and an epilogue.[2] Stated as strategies for believing and living amid crisis, each of these nine sections encourages us to take heart and to act faithfully toward God. Taken together, these dramatic scenes encouragingly remind us that our basic vision and values—when lived consistently—bring victory. In Revelation, the vision revolves around an unshakable confidence that God can overcome any crisis. The corresponding values reflect an unquenchable optimism that believers can grow—even in broken times. As in Revelation, our vision and values undergird our ability to lead strategically when our world becomes chaotic.

Take Heart: God's in Charge

Prologue's Vision and Value: In crisis, take heart by remembering that Christ, who spans time completely as One who was, is, and is to come, is ultimately in charge of history (Revelation 1:1-8). Revelation's prologue warns ominously of "what must soon take place" (Revelation 1:1) but urges Christians to take heart (Revelation 1:3).

While in a Nazi concentration camp, Viktor Frankl learned one of life's deepest lessons. Even amid life's extremes, if you and I have a *why* to life, we can endure almost any *what*.[3] When we know God is in charge of the world, we can take heart and live with serenity.

Take Heart: Evaluate Effectiveness

Act One/Vision and Value: In crisis, take heart and help your church evaluate the effectiveness of its ministry (Revelation 1:9–3:22). The curtain goes up on Act One by presenting John as "a companion in the suffering" and by counseling "patient endurance" (Revelation 1:9 NIV). Then, the seven churches of Asia are evaluated with praise and appreciation for faithful service as well as with prescribed actions for lapses in faith and service (Revelation 2:1–3:22).

Congregations may be the least evaluated institutions in our society (though pastors might consider themselves the most vulnerable to incessant personal evaluation). Christians seem to forget that church leaders are human and that ministries have a way of losing their edge over the course of time. Crisis often forces us to examine how we're doing in ministry. Wouldn't the world we minister in and to become a better place if we evaluated our effectiveness as a regular, strategic process?

Take Heart: God Has a Plan

Act Two/ Vision and Value: In crisis, take heart and look for God's plan in history (Revelation 4:1–8:1). The scene switches in Act Two from earth to heaven—to God's throne room with the Lamb who is worthy to open the seven seals. There, in spite of war, famine, martyrdom, and natural catastrophe, the redeemed of the ages announce triumphantly, "Salvation belongs to our God, who is seated on the throne, and to the Lamb!" (Revelation 7:10).

Some people seem to have a sense of destiny and appear to know their place in God's broader plan. They view life through a wider lens and see that they fit into a larger picture. When a skinny rookie baseball player came up for his first major league at bat with the Milwaukee Braves, the opposing catcher chided Hank Aaron that he was holding the bat incorrectly. The catcher observed that the bat's brand couldn't be read and that was wrong. Aaron, the man who became the greatest home run hitter in professional baseball history thought over the catcher's complaint and answered calmly, "I didn't come up here to read." Aaron knew what he was meant to do.

Take Heart: God Is with Us

Act Three/ Vision and Value: In crisis, take heart and know that God meets us amid everything life brings (Revelation 8:2–11:19). Act Three reveals a series of terrifying visions. In spite of an array of threatening possibilities, this act closes with glorious assurance, "The kingdom of the world has become the kingdom of our Lord and of his Messiah, and he will reign forever and ever" (Revelation 11:15). Consequently, the saints thank God for "rewarding your servants" (Revelation 11:18).

Knowing we're not alone in the face of stressful events gives us courage to face life confidently. When Donna Shalala was the president at Hunter College a decade ago, the administration offered midnight breakfast during finals week for students who were studying late into the night. President Shalala donned an apron and served meals. Some officials worried that the president was undercutting her authority by such menial work. Shalala disagreed. Instead, she saw this simple act as a way of making leaders real and of humanizing the institution. "I think knowing that someone cares that you do well on your exams is the message I should get across," affirms Donna Shalala.

Take Heart: It Isn't Over Yet

Act Four/ Vision and Value: In crisis, take heart but expect the conflict between good and evil to become intense and personal (Revelation 12:1–14:20). Act Four spotlights the source of Christians' persecution—the agents of evil. These persons "make war on . . . those who keep the commandments of God and hold the testimony of Jesus" (Revelation 12:17). A hideous beast was "allowed to make war on the saints and to conquer them" (Revelation 13:7). Amid this mortal combat, believers are called to "endurance" (Revelation 14:12).

Management theorists observe that, in organizations, layoffs shrink our self-esteem. When Illinois Bell was broken up by the court's antimonopoly order, some employees endured well while others buckled physically and emotionally. This stressful process was tracked by a team of mental health experts. Three "C's"—commitment, control, and challenge—made the difference. If people were committed to their work, felt a measure of control over their lives, and saw change as a natural challenge in the flow of life, they showed resilience and were described as "hardy executives."[4] Commitment, control, and challenge are all elements of and outlooks toward faith.

Take Heart: God Will Judge

Act Five/ Vision and Value: In crisis, take heart and be reminded that everyone and everything stands under God's judgment (Revelation 15:1–16:21). Act Five depicts severe plagues of judgment culminating in Armageddon. Yet, the eternal God retains his power (Revelation 15:5-8).

111

We all live under God's indictment and count on his forgiveness for second chances. When Fiorello La Guardia was mayor of New York City, he tried to understand how government was functioning by filling in for officials in various municipal departments. One cold winter evening La Guardia presided over Night Court. A man was brought before him who was charged with stealing a loaf of bread to feed his starving family. La Guardia made no exceptions and fined the man ten dollars. Then, in an unusual act of grace, the mayor reached into his own pocket and handed the court's clerk a ten dollar bill to pay the offender's fine. Further, La Guardia fined everyone in the courtroom fifty cents for living in a city where a man had to steal bread in order to stave off starvation for his family. The bailiff collected $47.50 for the defendant who used it to buy groceries for his family.

Take Heart: God Will Win

Act Six/ Vision and Value: In crisis, take heart and watch as God confronts evil (Revelation 17:1–20:10). The whore of Babylon appears and becomes drunken on the blood of the saints in Act Six. But God defeats the prostitute "who corrupted the earth with her fornication, and he has avenged on her the blood of his servants" (Revelation 19:2).

The Bible depicts God as an initiator. When God takes action in the face of evil, he ultimately overcomes the forces of evil. This pattern of Divine triumph impresses believers and assures us that we too will find spiritual victory as a reward for faithfulness. Remember the affirmation of Romans?

> All things work together for good for those who love God, who are called according to his purpose. . . . in all these things we are more than conquerors through him who loved us. For I am convinced that neither death, nor life, nor angels, nor rulers, nor things present, nor things to come, nor powers, nor height, nor depth, nor anything else in all creation, will be able to separate us from the love of God in Christ Jesus our Lord. (Romans 8:28-39)

Take Heart: God Will Make New

Act Seven/ Vision and Value: In crisis, take heart and anticipate God's new creation (Revelation 20:11–22:5). Final judgment unfolds in Act Seven. The new heaven and the new
Jerusalem demonstrate the power of God.

Martin Seligman's *Learned Optimism*[5] notes a vital contrast in
the ways we deal with crisis. Amid pressure, two ways of
viewing life emerge. Some persons learn helplessness, become
pessimistic, and give up under pressure; others learn hopeful-
ness, become optimistic and persevere. What makes the difference? Three perceptions provide the watershed when bad
things happen.

(1) Is this situation permanent or temporary? The pessimist
fears the circumstance will persist and blames his lack of ability
for the problem. "Always" and "never" fill his conversation,
and the hurt is expected to remain forever. In contrast, the
optimist feels the problem will pass with time and effort.
"Sometimes" and "lately" provide the time frame for this particular issue. The hurt will go away soon.

(2) Is this situation universal or specific? The pessimist believes that bad events have universal causes while good events
have specific causes. Therefore, she experiences helplessness in
many areas of life, feels doomed, and often gives up when she
fails. On the other hand, optimists believe bad events have
specific causes but good events have universal causes. Consequently, any helplessness she feels is limited to the troubled
area only. Optimists pick themselves up, dust themselves off,
and march on in the face of failure.

(3) Who's responsible for this situation? Pessimists feel that
good things come from others and don't like themselves as
much; optimists feel good things come from within themselves
and like themselves more.

Overall, optimistic persons achieve more, are less depressive,
enjoy better health, and have more fun in life. Not surprisingly,
religious faith is a key factor in changing our life stance from
pessimism to optimism.[6]

Take Heart: God Will Vindicate

Epilogue's Vision and Value: In crisis, take heart and realize that Christ has the last word (Revelation 22:6-21). The epilogue assures believers that Christ is coming soon to vindicate his followers. In response, John invites, "Maranatha," or "Come, Lord Jesus" (Revelation 22:20).

Matthew Arnold once lamented that his historical era was "caught between two worlds—one dead and the other powerless to be born." The final paragraph of Revelation also depicts a similar "two world" situation—one being defeated and the other being birthed through the power of God. That vision lends courage to the believer who is merely trying to survive amid crisis.

Even with victory assured, there's an implicit warning in the last few sentences of Revelation. Crisis circumstances can completely intimidate leaders, causing us to ignore what's about to happen and to miss the opportunity of responding to the new world. May the eyes of faith help us see when to close old doors and when to open new ones.

My Life Is Christ

At any given point in time, there are several dozen "hot spots" in our world where war or famine are raging and daily life is so out of control that survival is all that counts. The war in Bosnia is a tragic struggle for survival which has received considerable media attention. The suffering in that war-torn area is beyond imagining.

Mr. Teufik Cerovic, a recent Christian convert from Islam, has written a touching letter to American friends describing both hardship and faith related to the Bosnia situation. In spite of the strife, he is at work establishing a Christian church in the old Muslim section of Sarajevo. Mr. Cerovic agonizes:

> It has already started to get cold here. Our apartment is an "ice factory." I am worried about how we can survive over this third cold winter. We are naked and barefoot! Our wardrobes are

empty, there is no electricity or water. May God help us! My desire is to live normal for just one month, to eat until I am full, to take a bath, to just once feel human. This is . . . a dream . . . I dream.

In the midst of this chaos, Mr. Cerovic's dream of a better day enables him to see a redemptive pattern at work even amid war and ethnic cleansing. He adds:

to me it is the greatest joy that our faith in Jesus can grow and that people . . . turn to the Lord. These are the greatest riches. Everything else is unimportant and passing away. My life is Christ. . . . My tears which now fall while I am writing this letter are of joy because I know that Christ lives in me.

Mr. Cerovic echoes the spirit of Revelation. God holds the world in his hands and will care for his own. In the midst of crisis, when survival is the only agenda, believers in Christ encourage each other in the faith that our ministries can remain focused, flexible, and future-oriented. That's feasibility strategy at its best.

— 9 —
A Primer in Crisis Survival

Too often, we allow crises to point us toward preliminary questions rather than ultimate ones. For example, we inquire of others, "What happened to you?" Instead, we should ask, "What did you do with what happened to you?" That's the real question for leaders amid crises. Strategic response and responsibility are more important than mere action and reaction, where crisis is concerned.

Crises occur. The tension is not "if" we will experience crisis but "when." Since crisis is inevitable, leaders must prepare to set the pace, create strategy, and choose tactics when we face a "broken time" akin to the era of the book of Revelation.

Understanding Crisis

Crisis is frightening. By definition, crisis is that fluid, unsettled, and unsettling phase in personal and organizational life when some decisive change is emerging. Massive uncertainty engulfs persons and organizations when crisis is the state of affairs. For many leaders and organizations, crisis is a make-or-break era when the present and the future of personal and institutional life are shaped in new ways.

Crises aren't optional, unfortunately. Periodically, life generates a crisis for us. The old statement that death and taxes are the only sure things in life is true—only if death and taxes are clearly defined as major league crises. Are we prepared for the inevitable? If not, how can we think strategically about crisis?

How can leaders manage crisis? The Three Mile Island near-catastrophe is a case study in crisis management that left important lessons behind. Steven Fink served on Pennsylvania's crisis management team during the unfolding situation at the nuclear reactor. Fink's *Crisis Management: Planning for the Inevitable* helpfully describes the "anatomy of a crisis."[1]

According to Fink's observations, crises move through four identifiable stages.

(1) The *Warning Stage* of a crisis presents small, seemingly insignificant signs that collectively point toward an impending disaster. These tiny omens serve as "prodromes," from the Greek expression meaning "running before." To use Jesus' reminder, only those who have "eyes that see" will take any notice of these early warning signals and sense a precrisis state of affairs.

———————— ⊕ ————————

High

I M P A C T	GATHERING STORM	THUNDER AND LIGHTENING
	CLOUDS ON THE HORIZON	DRIPPING WATER

Low   High

PROBABILITY

If crisis is thought of as a weather front, a "barometer" to measure the cumulative features of the "impact of the crisis" coupled with the "probability of the crisis occurring" offers one way to diagnose the prodrome. When "impact" is matched to "probability," emerging crises can be identified by type with "clouds on the horizon" the least threatening "weather front" and "thunder and lightning" the most ominous of the four possibilities.

(2) The *Avalanche Stage* features swift and intense change and occurs when the crisis has erupted. The point of no return has been passed. Swift, sure response is required to meet the demands of the situation and to minimize the long-term damage a full-blown crisis may cause.

With the "war games" flavor of stage 2, action rather than analysis is the appropriate response. At this stage, leaders don't have the luxury of "why" questions. There are only three inquiries appropriate to the Avalanche Stage: What plans have we made? How can we implement these plans? When can we put them into effect? In the midst of "thunder and lightning," we take cover and act as swiftly and wisely as we can under the circumstances.

(3) The *Post-Mortem Stage* is the chronic phase of crisis. It can linger indefinitely and is usually measured by fallout. How are the people and the organization responding? Are there plaudits for leaders who stepped forward and faced the crisis constructively? Has some recovery and healing occurred? Or is there still a path of destruction, leaving people and organizations in the debris? Are people still in a state of doubt and self-analysis? Is the organization regaining its footing and beginning to look toward the future?

(4) The *Resolution Stage* incorporates new insights before returning to "business as usual" until the next crisis. At this stage, any learnings and changes for leaders and the overall organization are put into practice as preventive measures. Contingency-

based planning, building on the facts and the "what if's" of the previous crisis episode, is now necessary if future crises are to be met with more resilience. This stage moves deliberately beyond the "What happened to you?" question to the "What did you do with what happened to you?" response.

Content and Mechanics: a Crucial Separation

Successful crisis management calls for the ability to separate the content of the crisis from the mechanics of the crisis. At Three Mile Island, panic became the content of the crisis, while shutting down a nuclear reactor provided the mechanics of the situation. In Revelation, the content of the crisis focused on the believers' hope in Christ while the mechanics dealt with coping with the realities of persecution and threat. When content and mechanics are sorted out, an effective plan can be designed, allowing leaders to act early and flexibly on the crucial content of the crisis. With a crisis management plan, two critical actions can be taken: structure and interpretation. (1) Structure helps us cope with anxiety and uncertainty—that's part of the genius of a plan for dealing with the mechanics of crisis. (2) Then, the emotional components of crisis can be faced with a surer hand because content is ultimately the deeper issue of leaders' concern.

The most telling aspects of the Three Mile Island incident— and most crises—dealt with fear and disclosure. Here's a rule of thumb for leaders amid crisis: the fear of the unknown creates an emotional crisis, but the fear of truth creates a spiritual crisis. For religious leaders, we must deal with both the emotional and spiritual components of crisis. Therefore, we must face crisis with both personal and professional calm and curiosity as well as an unswerving commitment to truth and to the disclosure of information. Congregations become spooked amid crisis— especially when the content-laden dimensions of crisis become paramount and the emotional and spiritual issues reign.

The Doors of Crisis

Crisis has a way of battering down the doors of our personal and congregational lives. For example, congregations have at least three doors for crises to enter. The "front door" or entry points of a church provide for congregational growth. While growth crises are nice problems to face, boom growth can generate unsettling challenges for churches. The "back door" or exit points can also shake up a church when morale crashes and many members leave.

The "trap door" or personal emergencies members encounter begin as individual traumas but can mushroom into organizational dilemmas when the crisis has an impact on the congregation's psyche and becomes system wide. Trap door emergencies remind us why the Chinese word for crisis uses two symbols—one for "danger" and another for "opportunity." Crisis is always two-sided, fraught with danger and brimming with opportunity.

Before, During, After

Crisis has "before," "during," and "after" phases. Each phase contains its own challenges for leaders. "Before," when examined strategically, is a prime time to focus with flexibility on the future. That is, "before" is a strategic formulation opportunity. "During" boils down to stress management. Leaders guard themselves and their group against overload by applying emotional, spiritual, and physical resources to stressors. "After" deals with survivor issues and is informed by posttraumatic research insights from war, catastrophe, and major life disruptions.

One of the crises confronting persons and organizations in our contemporary world is the phenomenon of downsizing. Laid-off workers and shrinking institutions both become infected with "survivor sickness."[2] Grieving properly and empowering persons with a core purpose are two handles on the separation process, resulting from this painful trapdoor experience. David Noer's *Healing the Wounds* is a creative resource for treating the survivors of crisis.

What Crisis Can Teach Us

The lessons of crisis are powerful, especially when crisis is seen as "intensified opportunity" to learn some of life's deepest secrets. When I review the final days of Jesus' life and ministry to see how he dealt with crisis, four themes leap off the pages of the New Testament record for me. First, spiritual renewal remains central. The Last Supper and Gethsemane are intensified opportunities to recharge spiritual batteries. Second, a support network is critical. The Twelve certainly aren't perfect as encouragers, but they provide some companionship for the intensified opportunity of crisis. Third, our core values are clarified during crisis. The conversation in Mark 10:35-45 and the experience of Gethsemane reduce life to its basics. Last, I'm impressed that Jesus never shows signs of panic or of forfeiting his integrity. When others are losing their composure, he never loses his presence. Renewal and worship, communion, serenity, and a sense of roots are baseline resources for facing life's extremes.

Let's sum up some of the foundational lessons from crisis situations. What can we learn from crisis?

(1) Crisis reduces life to its basics. An Englishman, convicted of treason and sentenced to be hanged, remarked with typical British understatement, "When you know you're going to be hanged in a fortnight, it focuses your mind wonderfully." In extreme situations, we are forced to refocus our lives on what's really central to our hearts and souls. We distill out the critical few important elements of our lives and filter them away from the trivial many distractions in our lives. Compromise is less likely when we know clearly who we are and what we stand for. (2) Crisis becomes a survival exercise. It makes us simplify our lives and travel light. Personally and organizationally, we pare down to the bare essentials. Crisis leaves no room for luxury. So, crisis reminds us what's worth sacrificing for. One of the saints of the church was asked what he would do if he

knew he would die the next morning. He replied that he would eat his supper, say his prayers, and go to sleep.

(3) Crisis awakens us and opens our pores to possibilities. We are pushed to see new options and consider fresh alternatives. The anxiety and stress of extreme circumstances whittle away the callouses we've developed on our imaginations during times when creativity was somewhat more optional. Crisis increases our emotional and spiritual agility.

(4) Crisis evokes discipline. What doesn't kill me makes me stronger. Amid crisis, we build endurance, toughen ourselves, and commit ourselves to survive. Athletes used to apply a product called Tufskin ointment to areas that were apt to blister during training or competition. The result was instant callouses, allowing them to perform with more physical and mental consistency.

(5) Crisis drives us back to our central support group. We find how crucial encouragement is during broken times. Revelation is a book that brims over with encouragement in the midst of life-and-death struggles.

(6) Crisis helps us discover grace and become more graceful. When crisis is viewed as intensified opportunity, our eyes are often opened to see the work of God in our lives, our core values, and the importance of encouragers. Grace is everywhere. That discovery helps us recognize grace and be more graceful in the face of difficulty.

(7) Crisis spotlights meaning in our lives. During the Holocaust, some Jews in the Nazi concentration camps prayed for Allied bombs to fall directly on them. Was this a suicide fantasy, a way to escape suffering? The survivors who have reported this phenomenon claim they were willing to sacrifice their lives if necessary to destroy the ovens that were the death houses for so many of their companions. Meaning may have been sparse under those extreme circumstances, but it was not extinguished. Meaning identifies what's vital to us; meaning roots us in the elements of our lives that give us hope and keep our eyes on the horizon.

(8) Crisis calls some of us to leadership. The four horsemen of the Apocalypse (Revelation 6:1-8)—war, peace taking, famine, and death—create the most extreme crises; they jar doors open so that leaders can step forward. And they do. John Gardner asserts that the American Revolution produced great leaders precisely because the times were extreme.[3] The crises of broken times invite persons to take the risks of leadership.

Using Survivor's Flashbacks

Revelation shows leaders three dimensions of strategy in the midst of crisis. Decide to survive. Encourage each other. Commit yourself to return to your life's focus with flexibility and a future-orientation.

Amid chaos, how can leaders center themselves again and review their direction? The "3R" approach offers a flashback approach to surviving crisis:

Use the first "R" to *remind* yourself of your strategic focus. The kingdom of God isn't a passing fad; it provides an ongoing, eternal target for strategic leadership.

Use the second "R" to *react* flexibly to the challenges as well as the opportunities inherent in the crisis. Learn the lessons from crisis thoroughly.

Use the third "R" to *rehearse* your future. Visualize your goal even when the pressure you feel pushes you to deal only with the present. Leaders deal in tomorrows even when today threatens to engulf us with its pressures and cares.

Committing to the Future

Survival isn't a dirty word. Amid crisis, leaders do what's feasible to weather the storm and to return to a new result-resource-risk cycle. A resilient commitment to God's kingdom helps us look beyond the immediate to the future.

FAITH

The Strategic
Use of Imagination

— 10 —
The Art of
Strategic Thinking

Thinking strategically is a labor-intensive enterprise of imagination. That is, the craft of strategy, like any artistic endeavor, requires discipline and hard work in order to be creative. Listen to General George Patton's description of the background work required for the kind of strategic thinking he applied before he faced the Germans in World War II:

> I have studied the enemy all my life. I have read the memoirs of his generals and his leaders. I have even read his philosophers and listened to his music. I have studied in detail the account of every . . . one of his battles. I know exactly how he'll react under any given set of circumstances. And he hasn't the slightest idea what I'm going to do. So when the time comes, I'm going to whip . . . him.[1]

Patton, like most leaders, realized that disciplined, imaginative thinking is necessary for strategic effectiveness. Fortunately for those of us in ministry leadership, the art and science of strategic thinking involves the same kinds of thought patterns that help us think theologically.

Leader as Jazz Musician

Too frequently, thinking is described mostly as stationary, straight-line, lockstep problem solving. In this scenario the facts from the past are extended into the present; they are built on as we move from where we are to where we'd like to go. The cognitive task is seen as simple—read the notes, play the notes.

127

But, strategic thinking is more jazzlike,[2] more improvisational, more a group effort than "by-the-(song)book" problem solving. Strategic thinking anticipates what's around the bend; it's mobile, curved, "ad-lib," impromptu solution finding. Strategists live by their wits and intuition as much as by the facts.

Strategic thinking certainly isn't dumb luck. Some "lucky" leaders seem to subscribe to the "Christopher Columbus Approach to Strategy." They claim that Columbus discovered America mostly by accident. Consequently, they draw hope from three facts. (1) When Columbus left, he didn't know where he was going. (2) When he arrived, he didn't know where he was. (3) When he returned, he couldn't tell where he'd been. In spite of Columbus's good fortune, effective strategists are willing to pay the price in effort and creativity to "write history in advance." They use their hearts, their heads, and their feel for the future.

Brain Power for Strategic Thinking

How human beings solve problems has been of interest of to philosophers and scientists for centuries. When primitive surgery was first attempted, physicians noted that the human brain has two hemispheres. Continuing observation and research showed that the two hemispheres operated in distinctively different ways. The left hemisphere functions in a more logical, sequential, cause-effect fashion, while the right hemisphere operates with a more associative, relational, stream-of-consciousness approach. Consequently, it became fashionable to refer to persons as "left-brained" or "right-brained." As important as these distinctions are, recent neuroscience breakthroughs have shown that the hemispheric understandings of the brain are too simplistic.[3]

Neurologists and cognitive psychologists have recently discovered that the back of the brain and the front of the brain also function in distinctive manners. The back of the brain has been found to excel at sensory-oriented, here-and-now, "what is," tactical learning and thinking. On the other hand, the front of the brain provides big picture, future-oriented, "what if," strategic learning and thinking. The upshot of these insights is that we now know our brains aren't hemispheric. Rather, our brains are quadrantal with each of the four regions or zones featuring distinctive manners of solution finding. No matter which region of the brain we personally emphasize, we are all "smart" in our own way.

Our brain's quadrants team up and interact to learn, decide, and find solutions in almost magical ways. Our back brains provide facts, and our front brains generate frameworks for the facts. This "three-pound universe" is a divinely designed gold mine for strategists. Although everyone has strategic thinking abilities, leaders who emphasize front-brain thinking probably find strategic thinking especially comfortable. Left-front brain thinkers are adept at structured strategy formulation, while right-front brain thinkers generate relational strategy formulations with relative ease.

Most strategic enterprises call for the best features of every ounce of that enchanted loom we call our brain. For instance, when the engineers and planners designed America's space program, they thought strategically in "whole brain" fashion. To accomplish their goal of landing an astronaut on the moon, they first located the moon. That is, they identified their big picture target for the future. Then, they thought backwards to the earth and designed their process with a dizzying myriad of measures and equations and facts. "Find the moon and think back to the earth" is an accurate metaphor for strategic thinking.

What are the various elements of strategic thinking? What are the pieces of the solution-finding process? At least seven elements of a leader's strategic thinking process are identified and described below.

Strategy Generations over Time

First, strategy thinking fits into its organization's current stage. Here at the end of our exploration of the basic elements of leadership strategies, we've identified the natural, sequential development of four stages or generations of ministry strategies through the New Testament. Each generation applies unique strategies to its special challenges.

The ministry launch strategies of Jesus and the Gospels are focused and foundational; they reflect the inaugurating approaches typical of persons who launch great enterprises. First-generation strategies are highly selective; they build on fresh visions, establish a central home base, and function within the "now" of an immediate time horizon. These leadership initiatives are illustrative of paradigm shifters. The challenge of first-generation strategists is to focus narrowly and think the unthinkable, or, at least to think about radically new options.

The second-generation missionary strategies of Acts and the fledgling churches are flexible and expansionistic—without losing their focus. The entrepreneurial zeal of the missionary impulse frequently widens the boundaries of ministry within a near-term, or "soon," time horizon. These leadership approaches are typical of paradigm pioneers. The challenge of second-generation strategists is to do what hasn't been done before, or at least to try what hasn't been fully attempted.

The Pastoral Epistles have the flavor of a more conserving spirit common to third-generation strategies. Third-generation strategists struggle with the future. Their risk is that they will attempt to make tomorrow just like yesterday. At this stage, roles become more defined and organizations take on more permanent forms. During the third generation, strategists preserve gains and look toward a somewhat longer-term, "then" time horizon.

Third-generation strategists attempt their leadership from an established base typical of paradigm preservers. Although third-generation strategists may find themselves tempted to become overly cautious, they have an obligation to be open to God's new paradigms in missions and ministry. These leaders enjoy the possibility of becoming the movers and shakers of the next movement in the faith. Their challenge is to renew the machine before it ossifies into monuments to yesterday. Otherwise, third-generation strategists may slide into a preservationist mind-set and settle for defensive ministries and institutions.

Revelation shows us how to cope with crises—from a strategic perspective. Fourth-generation strategists cope with what's feasible or possible, given the limits of crisis circumstances. To confront higher anxiety levels in the organization, leaders deal with structures for survival, encouragement, and recommitment to a fresh cycle of strategy development. These paradigm revisers are willing to move quickly to stabilize the organization and then redirect their energies toward keeping the main thing the main thing.

Effective strategists know their times, organizationally speaking. They carefully and deliberately match strategic initiatives to the needs of their organization.

Strategy and Life Stage

Second, strategic thinking is inescapably personal, reflecting leaders' own life situations. The age and stage of strategists' lives flavor the advantages they feel they have in ministry. Personal "mileage" and maturity make a difference; energy level can become a watershed. Younger people sometimes don't know their limits or even recognize their mortality; older people are more apt to be keenly aware of both of these limitations and the stark fact that they won't live forever. In a way, the lessons of midlife often force strategy shifts. When young adult energy is traded for middle adulthood's experience, strategic shifts are likely. Living a "no limits" life during our twenties and thirties can fray our lives at the edges and bring about what Harry Emerson Fosdick described as a "frittered life" and a new set of life strategies.

We have a biblical example of how life stage affects ministry strategy. Paul's mellowing with age may well account for his switch from a more general, "all things" strategy (1 Corinthians 9:22) in his earlier ministry to a more targeted, "one thing" outlook (Philippians 3:13) during his middle adulthood in a prison cell. The passage of time and the narrowing of opportunities may have switched Paul from many interests to mini-interests.

Hear the strategic redirection in Paul's words: "But this one thing I do: forgetting what lies behind and straining forward to what lies ahead, I press on toward the goal for the prize of the

THE "GENERATIONS" OF STRATEGY

JESUS	ACTS	PASTORALS	REVELATION
FIRST	SECOND	THIRD	FOURTH
LAUNCH	EXPAND	ESTABLISH	SURVIVE
FOCUS	FLEXIBILITY	FUTURE	FEASIBILITY
PARADIGM SHIFTERS	PARADIGM PIONEERS	PARADIGM PRESERVERS	PARADIGM REVERSERS
NOW	SOON	LATER ...	YESTERDAY!!!

heavenly call of God in Christ Jesus" (Philippians 3:13-14). Paul had acquired a track record. He had successes and failures to put behind him if he intended to sprint toward the finish line God had drawn in the dust before him.

Some persons have difficulty setting their past successes aside in order to seize the future. For example, in one of my early pastorates, a former college homecoming queen tried to stave off midlife by spending four hours each day on makeup. Although still an attractive woman, she was so fixed on one golden Saturday in a long distant October that she was missing her future. On the other side of the ledger, some folks can't shake off the psychic scars of past failures and move on with life. Paul successfully laid aside the pluses and minuses of his remarkable yesterdays in order to pursue an even better tomorrow. Adopting new life strategies at midlife is one way to avoid obsolescence.

Effective strategists also realize their strategic options are influenced by where they are personally in the human life cycle. We all carry our individual history with us, affecting what we value and how we see the future.

Strategy and Innovation

Third, strategic thinking is always an innovative process. Effective strategists are able to stretch boundaries in order to free themselves to discover new options. They question everything and color outside the lines. They refuse to allow sacred cows to block their access to breakthrough ideas. Innovators play at least four roles as they strategize.[4] (1) As explorers they search for raw materials—the surprising bits, pieces, and connections of creativity. (2) As artists, they experiment with ideas and options by looking at them sideways or upside down and asking "What if . . . ?" (3) As judges, they weigh evidence and alternatives critically. (4) As warriors, they fight to make their innovative dreams come true. Innovation is, of course, a major ingredient of strategy formulation, especially in second-generation flexibility.

Effective strategists think creatively. They push back the barriers of innovation in order to discover and apply the freshest strategies they can find.

Strategy and Targets

Fourth, strategic thinking selectively chooses its targets. Finite resources, overwhelming opportunities, or flagging energy trigger the strategic process. When responsibilities outstrip resources, strategy becomes our way to survive and thrive. Consequently, strategists stay close to their core focus, especially first-generation strategy developers.

Effective strategists have an uncanny ability to zero in on the essence of the situation. They aren't easily distracted by the peripheral or the secondary or the trivial.

Strategy and Interaction

Fifth, strategic thinking is "bubble up" rather than "trickle down" thinking. Strategists appreciate the ideas and interaction of their organization's base of participants and its key stakeholders alike. Strategists believe good ideas "rub off" on each other and stimulate even better ideas in the interaction. Strategy is, after all, a grass-roots team sport—both in its creation and application, in its incubation and implementation.

Effective strategists think "we," not "I." While maintaining their freedom to define themselves apart from their group, strategists don't forget that they are a part of their group. They know that "two heads are better than one" when strategy is being formulated and that "the more the merrier" is necessary when strategy must be implemented.

Strategy and Contribution

Sixth, strategic thinking is detective work. Strategists are keenly aware of their own strengths. Likewise, they know what others excel at too—both their partners and their competitors.

Strategists match needs and resources in a process of investigative imagination.

Effective strategy is "hard-boiled," to use a phrase from the detective movies of the 1930s and 1940s. That is, strategists are relentless at reading themselves and others. Then, they see who can "crack the case" by making the pivotal contribution to the process.

Strategy and Mysticism

Seventh, strategic thinking for religious leaders centers on what God is doing in our lives, our religious communities, and our world. Prayer, Bible study, and interchange with a disciplined community of faith feed the sensitivity needed to think in harmony with the mystical dimension of strategy. God's activity in our lives tunes us to the hearts of others, to the response points in our leadership situations and settings, and to the motivating heritage of our group.

Effective strategists are mystics. They depend on God to help them see things that haven't quite materialized yet and to hear the melodies before most of their contemporaries even suspect there's music in the air. Strategists cultivate an intuitive sensitivity to what's emerging, an appreciation of what's yet to appear, and an ear for rhythms still to be composed.

Musical Metaphors for Strategists

Experts in communication and advertising claim that hearing is our most important sense. They concentrate on sounds; they use rhymes, jingles, slogans, and songs to present their messages effectively. In our reading of the New Testament, we have heard it echo with the sounds of strategy. Imagine the New Testament is a song about leadership strategy; note the pattern apparent in the music.

In the New Testament, Jesus is the Composer. He wrote the song, establishing the focus and laying down the baseline. Acts improvises on the theme and experiments with flexible variations. In fact, the leaders of Acts were the jazz musicians of

New Testament strategy. The Pastoral Letters play the song straight; they concentrate on note-by-note accuracy and functionality. These three epistles center on getting the song right—and preserving it. The Revelation could be a dirge amid a firestorm of persecution; instead, it plays a lullaby of comfort and encouragement for us.

From focus to flexibility to future-orientation to feasibility, we have listened to four verses of this song about leadership strategy unfold before our ears from the pages of the New Testament. Focus, flexibility, future, and feasibility form the theme song for Christian leadership strategists. It's a simple melody worth singing over and over again.

The ABCs of Strategy

Focus. Flexibility. Future. These three issues are key levers for leaders' strategic edge. Consequently, good leaders make thinking about focus, flexibility, and the future second nature. Occasionally, crisis forces a fourth, more temporary, strategic action: feasibility. Strategic leaders always focus with flexibility on the future; when necessary, they do what's feasible until they can return to a new strategic cycle. That's the formula for your "leading edge" in effective strategy.

Quick or Dead

There's an important lesson to be learned from the study of leadership strategy in the New Testament. God is an "on purpose" God who acts strategically for our redemption. When we follow God and model our lives, leadership, and ministries on God, we will think and act imaginatively, purposefully, strategically, and redemptively too. We will help congregations and other ministry groups discover and use well their advantages for ministry and missions. Our complicated times demand it. Our varied ministry opportunities demand it. Our Lord, the Master Strategist, demands it. Our models of biblical leadership demand it.

Effective leadership strategists have always been imaginative, flexible-thinking, and fast-acting. Given the pace and pressures at the end of the twentieth century, above all others, Christian leaders must be especially wise strategists. If we are to leaven our culture and change our world, we have no other choice. In our future world and in our future churches, there will be only two kinds of leaders: the quick and the dead. As strategic thinkers, may God grant us quickness!

NOTES

1. The Edge—Where and How Leadership Happens

1. Bruce D. Henderson, "The Origin of Strategy," *Harvard Business Review*, November–December 1989, 139-43.
2. Brian Steel Wills, *A Battle from the Start* (New York: Harper Collins, 1992), 1-3.
3. Tom Peters, *Liberation Management* (New York: Knopf, 1992), 575-76.
4. Tom Chappell, *The Soul of a Business: Managing for Profit and the Common Good* (New York: Bantam, 1993), xiv.
5. For insights on how artisans such as potters and carpenters may develop strategic thinking skills, see Henry Mintzberg, "Crafting Strategy," *Harvard Business Review* Reprint No. 87407 (1987), Harvard Business School Publishing Division, Boston, MA 02163 and Miyamoto Musashi, *A Book of Five Rings* (Woodstock, N.Y.: Overlook, 1974), 41-43.
6. A. M. Hunter, *Introducing New Testament Theology* (London, SCM, 1957), 13-14.
7. Arnold B. Rhodes, *The Mighty Acts of God* (Richmond: CLC, 1964), 253-65.
8. Thomas J. Peters and Robert H. Waterman, Jr., *In Search of Excellence* (New York: Harper & Row, 1982), 13-14.

2. Jesus: Focused Master Strategist

1. Søren Kierkegaard, *The Sickness unto Death*, trans. Alastair Hannay (London: Penguin, 1989), 62-63.
2. Edwin H. Friedman, *Generation to Generation* (New York: Guilford, 1985), 228-34.
3. C. S. Lewis, *The Great Divorce* (New York: Macmillan, 1946), 72.
4. Bruce D. Henderson, "The Origin of Strategy," *Harvard Business Review*, November–December 1989, 139-43.
5. Cited by Stephen A. Stumpf and Thomas P. Mullen in *Taking Charge: Strategic Leadership in the Middle Game* (Englewood Cliffs, N.J.: Prentice-Hall, 1992), 93.
6. Michel Robert, *Strategy Pure and Simple* (New York: McGraw-Hill, 1993), 52-53.
7. John H. McClanahan, *Man as Sinner* (Nashville: Broadman Press, 1987), 39.
8. Jean Kerr, *The Snake Has All the Lines* (New York: Crest, 1962), viii.
9. Robert, *Strategy Pure and Simple*, 99.

10. McClanahan, *Man as Sinner*, 47.
11. Karl Olsson, *Come to the Party* (Waco, Tex.: Word, 1972).
12. Robert K. Greenleaf, *Servant Leadership* (New York: Paulist, 1977), 7.
13. McClanahan, *Man as Sinner*, 47.
14. Quoted in Emmett C. Murphy and Michael Snell's book on modern leadership needs, *The Genius of Sitting Bull* (Englewood Cliffs, N.J.: Prentice-Hall, 1993), viii.
15. This is Wayne Oates' phrase for thought patterns that aren't healthy or productive.
16. Robert, *Strategy Pure and Simple*, 40-41.
17. Dietrich Bonhoeffer, *The Cost of Discipleship* (New York: Macmillan, 1963), 45-60.

3. Learning Focused Leadership

1. Stephen R. Covey, *The Seven Habits of Highly Effective People* (New York: Simon and Schuster, 1989), 95-144.

4. Acts: Flexible Leadership for Strategic Change

1. Joel Arthur Barker, *Paradigms: the Business of Discovering the Future* (New York: HarperBusiness, 1992), 32.
2. Ibid., 40.
3. Ibid., 41.
4. Thomas S. Kuhn, *The Structure of Scientific Revolutions* (Chicago: University of Chicago Press, 1970), 158.
5. Barker, *Paradigms*, 164.
6. Ibid., 163.
7. Wes Seeliger, *Western Theology* (Atlanta: Forum House, 1973).
8. While the strategy observations are mine, the interpretative approach on Acts I've found most helpful for leadership studies is Frank Stagg, *The Book of Acts: the Early Struggle for an Unhindered Gospel* (Nashville: Broadman, 1955).
9. Noted by F. F. Bruce in his *Commentary on the Book of Acts* (Grand Rapids, Mich.: Eerdmans, 1955), 131.
10. Norton Paley, "A Strategy for All Ages," *Sales and Marketing Management*, January 1994, 51-52.
11. William Barclay, *The Acts of the Apostles* (Philadelphia: Westminster, 1953), 11.
12. Doug Ferguson, "Wilkinson, Sooners Won Three Titles," *Richmond (VA) Times-Dispatch*, February 11, 1994, D5.
13. Kennon L. Callahan, *Effective Church Leadership* (San Francisco: Harper & Row, 1990), 3.

5. Adapting to Flexible Leadership

1. Rick Warren and Leonard Sweet, *The Tides of Change: Riding New Waves in Ministry*, Abingdon Audio (Nashville: Abingdon Press, 1995).
2. Victoria Shaw and Garth Brooks, "The River," in *Ropin' the Wind* (Nashville: Capitol Records, 1991).

3. Lee Butcher, *Accidental Millionaire: The Rise and Fall of Steven Jobs at Apple Computer* (New York: Paragon House, 1988).
4. C. W. Lewis, *Mere Christianity* (New York: Macmillan, 1943), 183.

6. Pastoral Epistles

1. Edward John Carnell, "Fundamentalism," *Handbook of Christian Theology*, ed. Marvin Halverson and Arthur A. Cohen (New York: World, 1958), 142-43.
2. Ernest E. Mosley, *Called to Joy* (Nashville: Convention, 1973).
3. Eugene H. Peterson, *Working the Angles: the Shape of Pastoral Integrity* (Grand Rapids, Mich.: Eerdmans, 1990), 1.
4. Flannery O'Connor, *The Habit of Being*, ed. Sally Fitzgerald (New York: Farrar, Strauss, Giroux, 1979), 81.
5. Warren Bennis, *On Becoming a Leader* (Reading, Mass.: Addison-Wesley, 1989), 41.
6. Joseph L. Badaracco and Richard R. Ellsworth, *Leadership and the Quest for Integrity* (Boston: Harvard Business School, 1989), 98.
7. Ibid., 100-101.

7. Keeping the Future Our Target

1. Alvin Toffler and Heidi Toffler, *Creating a New Civilization* (Atlanta: Turner Publishing, 1995), 21.
2. Rafael Steinberg, ed., *Man and the Organization* (New York: Time-Life Books, 1975), 8.
3. Some people develop a signature statement and become known for that single line. Comedian Jeff Foxworthy's book, *You Might Be a Redneck If . . .* (Atlanta: Longstreet Press, 1989), repeats the book's title over and over by defining "redneck" in dozens of funny ways.
4. Edwin B. Flippo, *Management: a Behavioral Approach* (Boston: Allyn and Bacon, 1970), 32.
5. Tom Peters, *Thriving on Chaos* (New York: Knopf, 1987).
6. Roger von Oech, *A Whack on the Side of the Head* (New York: Warner Books, 1983).

8. Revelation: When Survival Becomes the Agenda

1. Eugene H. Peterson, *Reversed Thunder: The Revelation of John and Praying Imagination* (San Francisco: Harper & Row, 1991).
2. Thomas S. Kepler, *Dreams of the Future* (Nashville: Abingdon Press, 1963), 61-63.
3. Viktor E. Frankl, *Man's Search for Meaning* (New York: Washington Square Press, 1959), 164.
4. Salvatore R. Maddi and Suzanne C. Kobasa, *Hardy Executives* (Chicago: Dorsey Professional Books, 1984).
5. Martin E. P. Seligman, *Learned Optimism* (New York: Alfred A. Knopf, 1991).
6. Seligman, 203-4.

9. A Primer in Crisis Survival

1. Steven Fink, *Crisis Management: Planning for the Inevitable* (New York: AMACOM, 1986).
2. David M. Noer, *Healing the Wounds: Overcoming the Trauma of Layoffs and Revitalizing Downsized Organizations* (San Francisco: Jossey-Bass, 1993).
3. John W. Gardner, *On Leadership* (New York: Free Press, 1990), 158.

10. The Art of Strategic Thinking

1. Quoted in Michel Robert, *Strategy Pure and Simple* (New York: McGraw-Hill, 1993), 88.
2. Max DePree, *Leadership Jazz* (New York: Doubleday, 1992).
3. An excellent resource for assessing how persons think is the Success Style Profile, a human resource development instrument designed, refined, and validated by Dennis E. Coates of Performance Support Systems of Newport News, Virginia. The SSP, a multifactor analysis of cognitive style, identifies—among other items—the emphasized region or regions in persons' unique ways of thinking.
4. Roger von Oech, *A Kick in the Seat of the Pants* (New York: Harper & Row, 1986).